BOOK COVER GRAPHIC

WASHINGTON, D.C. MORMON TEMPLE

Courtesy of Carol M. Highsmith

NO

MORMON FOR

PRESIDENT

[ITS THE PRIESTHOOD NOT THE CHURCH]

A BOOK FOR LAYMAN

BY DOUGLAS A. WALLACE

LCCN 2012911235

ISBN-13: 978-1466205130
ISBN-10: 146620513X

Printed by Create Space in the USA

A NEEDED ACKNOWLEDGEMENT:
[My Childhood Experience Like Paul's Experience on the Road to Damascus]

Author as 22 year old brainwashed Mormon Missionary
Preaching the "gospel" in Wales, UK 1951. He knew it all then.

Before going any further in this book, I am impressed to inform the reader that this work is the driven product of seventy two years of keeping within myself the aggregate notice of a commission or what I understood to be a mission given me as a child on my eighth birthday, May 8, 1937, from a source who I believed was the God of this world. That assertion is generally called a "fringe" event ridiculed by most people who have never had such an experience. I have to admit that after having had the experience I knew it would be ridiculed if I spoke of it. Other than knowing something had happened to me on that day in Ogden, Utah, details of it were forgotten and buried in the recesses of my mind. I just knew something strange had happened.

Lincoln Elementary, Ogden, Utah

I have documented that experience in my memoirs, *Under the Mormon Tree.*

On that day [May 8, 1937, Saturday 12:45 PM Mountain Standard Time], in a blinding light, a sudden presence of a personage who I spiritually knew presumably from a pre-life experience, then a conversation with an unseen voice speaking to me. I had just angrily shouted," God I know you are in there" as I passed a Mormon Church building a few blocks back [Ogden Eighth Ward] that I regularly attended.

The voice answered,"*I heard your prayer*". Prayer? I thought it was more like a cursing of God for the hurt I was then experiencing.

After a statement that He, [and I am assuming it was a "he" for I had been taught that God was a male person], did not dwell in structures made by the hand of man, particularly Mormon Temples, the message began with the leaders of the Mormon or LDS Church and the use of their temples as bait to unwitting followers.

Specifically, I was told that many years afterward in my life beginning in my late 40's, after a temple in Ogden, Utah had been built, I would be confronting those leaders over issues which concerned their quest to place the most senior survivor among them in a position of establishing a kingdom of god on earth with that individual and his successor(s) being crowned "king of the earth" supposedly representing the God of the Universe. I was told that would not be allowed and that I along with others would work to prevent that from happening. See Chapter 14 below for more detail.

That long suppressed experience was brought to light On April 6, 1976. The full story begins on page 139 of my memoirs.

As pointed out, I kept that event to myself for some 39 years and mostly beyond that until 2001 when I first posted my memoirs on the internet as an E-book. The truth was that I could only remember the event not the substance of it prior to April, 1976.

Living in a world where those kinds of experience are regarded as fringe, it takes a lot of sheer guts for me to make that statement. It is true however that I began my work in my late forties somewhat ignorantly as led by the spirit when I defied Mormon Church leaders in ordaining a black man to priesthood. A move which they duplicated two years later under a pretense of a revelation from God, doing the same but without apology to me or the many people they had destroyed who had held that intellectual position for years, particularly the intellectuals in Utah.

So I have been hanging around these past thirty four years to help prevent the Mormon Church from achieving open establishment of their "Kingdom of God on earth" which God has forbidden.

I was aware of that in 2007 when Mit Romney first ran for president. I began to poise myself to expose the dangers of his being elected president but when he dropped out the time was not yet appropriate.

Yet, today, as I look at the posture of the United States Government and its quest for empire, I am concerned that the so—called "war on terror" is but the beginnings of the surreptitious capture of the government by elements of the Melchizedek Priesthood placed in agencies of government doing the bidding of the Mormon prophet as the oaths taken in Mormon Temples. I am extremely concerned that the time is already too late to bring any effective halt to the ungodly scheme.

With that in mind, please read on and come to grips with the notion that the God of this universe could inform this writer as a child of the very issues which are now at a critical state of happening on planet earth even as we read and write.

As to the issue of seeing God [the Father] I make no claim but I claim to have seen a named personage in the midst of the light, whom I knew from a pre-life experience, which first drew my attention to return to the light. Thereafter it was a conversation with a voice from an unseen person in the light not the personage.

I honestly don't know if I would be doing this work in the absence of that experience. Yet I likely would have been guided by the spirit to this point in life

Please read on!

Doug Wallace

November 28, 2012

CONTENTS

INTRODUCTION.....13

PREFACE....14

PART ONE

1. Setting the Stage: Mormonism vs. Nazism... Page 24

2. How one gets brainwashed 33

3. How brainwashing is deepened 39

4. How it all got started 43

5. Who the Hell was Melchizedek? 49

6. Here cometh the priesthood! 52

7. Beware of men speaking as God 57

8. The law shall go forth from Zion 61

9. Zion in America......63

10. Mitt Romney as Manchurian candidate 73

11. What to expect if Romney is elected 80

12. A vote for Romney is a vote for Mormon Prophet

King.....87

PART TWO

13. Mormon Church leaders lie 94

CONTENTS-2

14. Mormon quest for empire: God's take on it 98

15. Holy Blood, Holy Grail 112

16. Huntsman or Romney? Choose your poison.........118

17. Obfuscating the Mormon Issue 122

18. Flying under the Radar 138

19 The National Security Agency: An Unholy Alliance 146

20. NSA Files on Americans Accessible to Mormon Church..153

21. The Sinister Entity behind the Façade of Mormonism 159

22. 9-11 and the Mormon-Mossad Connection......169

23. Monstrous Malignancy of the 1999 Church Handbook of Instructions ...177

24. Bringing Sense to Tax Exemption A coming Mormon Dilemma......183

25. The Mormon God: A Super Star Stud 189

26. The religious Empire: Public Enemy 194

CONTENTS-3

27. Lest Our Heads Get Swollen 201

28. Labels: Moslem, Christian, Jew......205

29. A New Year's Resolution for All Americans 209

30. Socialism is About People: Fascism is about 213
        Corporations

31. World Peace is Impossible without Spiritual 226
    Alignment

32. In God We Trust: A Blasphemous Statement ...226

33. The Lincoln-Douglas Debates and the Mormon
                Cancer Waiting on Mitt Romney, 232
34. Organized Religion: Hijacking Rights of Humans 240

35. Organized Religion: RICO Alamode?.......... 249

36. Religion: Sacred Cow of the Supreme Court...257

Collection of Letters regarding Utah NSA Data
                                Center....266
Defining Apocalypse................275

SUMMARY..........277

APPENDIX.........280   Wallace v. Romney Lawsuit.....282

"The leader who cannot adapt to external realities because he adheres to an internally programmed life script...has displaced his private needs upon the state."

Jerrold Post, M.D. Founder of CIA Center for Analysis of Personality and Political Behavior

INTRODUCTION:

Daily around the globe,
Inside Mormon Temples, [including the one pictured on
the book cover in Washington, D.C.,] dressed
In white ceremonial clothing
Mormon men and women by the thousands
Covenant to keep the "Law of Sacrifice".
In doing so, they,

"Covenant to sacrifice all that we possess, even our own lives if necessary, in sustaining and defending the kingdom of God."

The church [LDS] has been identified as the kingdom of god on earth [Mormon Doctrine pg 415]. It is claimed to be a political [physical] kingdom to conquer the world which will be shown in this book. Living and dying and even killing for the kingdom is a sacred covenant of Mormon Temple Initiates.

But remember, it is the priesthood known as the Melchizedek Priesthood [chapter 17] that is the real power behind the throne with the Mormon Prophet holding all priesthood keys sitting on the invisible throne

as Earth King

PREFACE

The history of the world is replete with instances of theocratic governments or governments controlled by religious notions which in turn control the masses under them with an iron fist. There is no authority like God in heaven to make men tremble before rulers especially when those rulers have brainwashed their subjects to believe that they are the elite of God. God and his rulers combined are fearsome!

Scattered throughout the earth are the bones of Homo sapiens who died in defending freedom from religious intolerances or who were slaughtered by theocratic despots because they refused to bow the knee or were convicted of offenses against God and/or the realm.

It was customary for rulers to become narcissistic allowing themselves to believe that because they had achieved supremacy, God had favored and blessed them. To offend them was thus an offence against God constituting blasphemy for which the penalty of death was appropriate.

The Christian world who praises King James for producing his ordered translation of the scriptures referred to as the KJV "Holy Bible" are little informed that he had Sir Walter Raleigh, the counselor and aide to Queen Elizabeth I put to death because he was an atheist! Because Raleigh did not believe in God, he could not be a devoted subject to James and thus was worthy of death.

This fate of Raleigh was not reported to we school children during our formative years in elementary education. We were only told tales such as his draping a shawl in the puddled gutter for Elizabeth to step on so that she would not get her feet wet! If Elizabeth was aware that Raleigh was an atheist, she never let on but rather used him to assist the Crown in its development of the New World in America. Indeed Raleigh, North Carolina was named after him. James, as successor to Elizabeth, on the other hand as with all despots ignored the valued contributions made by Raleigh to the British Empire but rather feared him as a non believer in James as the protectorate of God. After all if there was no God then James was an imposter!

Likewise throughout history many others have felt the severing edge of the sword or the searing heat of the stake when they were put to death for not believing exactly as expected by those in ecclesiastical authority. Witch hunts are a stain on New England and areas of Europe. Imagine burning a three year old girl at the stake!

Often times the forces on either side of a conflict are so deeply entrenched in opposing religious concepts that thousands die for no good reason. The Crusades are such a fine example of total idiocy that it makes one's body quiver in disgust to read such things as the children's crusade or what Richard the Lion hearted did to Jews living in Jerusalem when he attacked the city to dispel the control of the "Holy Land" from Muslims.

We are told that because of the urge for religious freedom, the Pilgrims sailed to America to establish themselves in a place where they could live their lives and religion without interference from the crown. We celebrate Thanksgiving Day each year in remembrance of that freedom and sought for religious liberty.

I am sure the heads of households offer a mealtime grace to God by the millions in America for that liberty.

Yet it was Pilgrim's Pride that threw Roger Williams out of New England because he developed a different view of religion. So freedom of religion is often thought of as a right to believe your way while at the same time being intolerant of others.

Scholars have known for centuries that religion has been the root cause of so much bitterness and hatred throughout the earth in known history and likely was before history was recorded. We may have discovered an exception to that by reason of research and studies made of the Pigmy civilization in central Africa which appears to have preceded the known Egyptian civilization some 3500 years BC. Pygmies had little or no crime and have never engaged in a war and yet believed or created the legend of the original Garden of Eden Genesis' story eons before Moses borrowed it for the benefit of creating a Hebrew culture.

We hear a lot these days from the religious right who want to vainly prove that the United States was founded as a Christian nation. Such thinking is without merit. Many founders not wishing to appear as atheists patterned themselves as **Deists**. That is they did not believe in the fall of Adam and reasoned since there was no fall per se, there was no need of a Christ Savior for redemption. George Washington was definitely one of them.

The mixing of religion with politics always will deny some if not all people of the right of freedom of religion. In truth freedom must of necessity be both inclusive and exclusive of religion. That is to say that freedom of religion has to grant the right of people to accept, modify **and** reject religion altogether. The right to accept religion without the right to reject religion is no right at all. Anything short of that is not freedom!

By this reasoning, proponents of religion of any variation have no right to interfere with the right to exclude religion as a guiding factor in one's life.

Nothing can be clearer than the statement that a total separation of religion and government is absolutely mandatory to peaceful rights of citizens.

Next to the Declaration of Independence, the article written by Jefferson and passed into law to separate religion and government by the state of Virginia was lauded as the second most notable drafting by Jefferson himself. It is worth quoting here:

A Bill for Establishing Religious Freedom, 1779

> Well aware... that all attempts to influence [the minds of men] by temporal punishments...tend only to beget hypocrisy and meanness...that the impious presumption of legislature and ruler, civil as well as ecclesiastical...hath established and maintained false religion over the greatest part of the world through all time;

> That to compel a man to furnish contributions of money for the promulgation of opinions which he disbelieves and abhors, is sinful and tyrannical.

> That even forcing him to support this or that teacher of his own religious persuasion is depriving him of liberty.

> That proscribing any citizen...unless he profess

or renounce this or that religious opinion, is dep-
riving him of a natural right,

That bribing with a monopoly of worldly
honours and emoluments those who will
externally profess and conform to....tends to
corrupt the principles of that very religion
it means to encourage.

[Therefore] We the General Assembly of Virginia
do enact that no man shall be compelled to
frequent or support any religious worship,
place, or ministry whatsoever...but that all men
shall be free to profess and by argument to
maintain, their opinions in matters of **religion**
and that the same shall in no wise diminish, enlarge,
or affect their civil capacities.

And we declare that the rights hereby asserted
are the natural rights of mankind, and that if
any acts shall be hereafter passed to repeal...or
narrow its operations, such will be an
infringement of natural right.

Jefferson's Bill speaks to the issue of religious freedom with a separation from government. That is government cannot compel its subjects to religion nor can religion as an organization compel government. To what extent personal religious beliefs may direct the actions of members of government is not addressed. Yet it would seem inherent in his bill that a formal religious organization cannot direct government because we would then have a theocracy which is clearly forbidden.

This book will examine the quest for empire both openly and covertly by the Church of Jesus Christ of Latter-day Saints better known as LDS and or the Mormon Church.

This book will demonstrate the fallacy of such quest in light of the right of religion by all persons as against theocratic control of peoples by the alleged "one and only true church upon the earth".

Mitt Romney and any other active Mormon male or female is so tainted with a belief in the control of the earth under the concepts held by so called Mormonism that he or they are a disgrace to democracy and to the precepts of religious freedom to the degree that they should never be allowed to be president of the United States of America.

The Constitution [Article VI paragraph 3 litmus test clause] states that there shall not be any religious test for candidacy to office in the Federal government and by extension of the Fourteenth Amendment to the states.

A litmus test being a condition of disqualifying a person because of his or her religious beliefs or some other condition or test. This is sound policy in a pluralistic society. This book is not intended to encourage any violation of that policy.

However, when we encounter a religious society that has at the root of its existence the notion that it is ordained of God to become the secular ruler of national and world government, it has overstepped its freedom of religion because, in effect, it has viewed itself as possessing a Divine right to politically rule with a theocratic club.

No such right exists or is compatible with the litmus test clause of Article VI of the U.S. Constitution.

This book will show that the nineteenth century American invented church known as the Church of Jesus Christ of Latter-day Saints commonly known as the Mormon Church is such a foreseen blight on freedom of religion that it poses a peril to the world should it be allowed to proceed with its goal of announcing that the Kingdom of God is now on earth with its Mormon Melchizedek Priesthood Leader crowned Earth King possessing authority to rule as Vice-Regent of Christ for a thousand years!

This book will also show that electing to the office of President of the United States a devout "Melchizedek Priesthood" holder such as Mitt Romney or any other Mormon will be done at the peril of democracy, religious freedom and the REPUBLIC itself!

As an attorney, I was required, under Article VI paragraph three, to be sworn to uphold and defend the Constitution. I have filed a lawsuit in Reno, Nevada U.S. District Court to address the constitutional issues posed by the Mitt Romney campaign. The irony here is that Article six paragraph three states,

"The Senators and Representatives before mentioned, and the Members of the several State Legislatures, and all executive and judicial Officers, both of the United States and of the several States, shall be bound by Oath or Affirmation, to support this Constitution; **but no religious Test shall ever be required as a Qualification to any Office or public Trust under the United States.**"

I am claiming standing to sue in the U.S. District court because of having taken the oath to defend the Constitution and that the court has jurisdiction over the subject matter with both issues arising out of a one sentence paragraph of Article six! The lawsuit is appended at the end of this book beginning at Page 282.

PART ONE

"THE PRIESTHOOD CAN EXIST WITHOUT THE CHURCH,

BUT THE CHURCH CANNOT EXIST WITHOUT THE PRIESTHOOD"

MORMON AXIOM

This is a distinction the reader needs to remember for it requires concentration to know that a Mormon High Priest such as Willard Mitt Romney would still be a High Priest of the Melchizedek Priesthood even if the Mormon Church were dissolved tomorrow.

Chapter 1

SETTING THE STAGE:

MORMONISM VERSUS NAZISM

[As strange/weird as that statement sounds there are parallels and differences]

If the reader is old enough to have lived at the time of the run up to World War II. He or she will have some concept of what I am about to discuss.

First let me say that several years after I had ordained Larry Lester to priesthood as per my memoirs, I became acquainted with two men who sought me out and whom I learned possessed physic abilities. The older man was a black American minister. The younger man, a lay minister, contacted me in early 1983 and advised me that he had two books which he had been prompted to give me. He informed me I needed to read them in order to be prepared for the future work I would be doing. One old used book he found and purchased, the other he Xeroxed at a library. What I am saying about Hitler and Nazism came from those two books I read nearly 30 years ago. After a domestic breakup I lost possession of the books. So what I am saying here comes strictly from memory.

Adolph Hitler came to power in 1933 at a time when Germany was suffering from the sanctions that had been imposed on it following World War One. Hitler started the Second World War by a false flag operation sending a massive military surging across the border with Poland in September 1939. He had an agreement with Joseph Stalin who simultaneously invaded Poland from the east. The Blitzkrieg [now called shock and awe as labeled by Donald Rumsfeld] crushed Poland in a few short days. Later Hitler would invade Russia and come very close to winning before the Russian winter destroyed his ambitions in the same manner that Napoleon experienced. Russia became an ally of the western forces until the end of the war in Europe. [Stalin did make a weak effort of the war in the Pacific by declaring war on Japan after the Nazis had collapsed].

For a few short years Hitler displayed an amazing precognitive ability to foresee victory when the whole of Europe except for the British Isles was under his heel. His Army commanders were amazed at how accurate his predictions for victory had been. That is why they allowed him to lead them in the beginning.

But after the June 1944 allied invasion it only took 11 months to deny him his victory. Had Hitler not misunderstood his precognitive abilities to see the future, he likely would not have been led down the path of self destruction as happened.

What may have been true visions of future events as they happened that he had "seen" which gave him a very big head, he failed to accept the negative vision of his defeat. As a result millions died.

This is the danger in precognitive abilities. What one "sees "of the future is not necessarily accurate and may or may not actually happen. He or she may be only picking up on what some future person creates as a mental image of a personal desire. Many so called prophets have had precognitive abilities but just because they "saw" them doesn't mean the world should rely on them or to attempt to bring about self fulfillment without reason.

Hitler had plans to establish what he called the Third Reich. It was intended that it would become the world government and control the earth for one thousand years. A thousand years of peace would reign or so he thought. A reign that would be representative of the period of peace prophesied by Biblical prophets. In other words the same goal that the Mormon Melchizedek priesthood is pursuing

It is noteworthy to know that peace can never be obtained in the absence of police/military action [see chapter 32].

The political party he organized, the National Socialist Party, or NAZI party, had a religious side. It was actually a religion disguised as a political party. Indeed the Nazi Party with its leader had ambitions of being the world fascist government.

Everyone is familiar with the movie, "Raiders of the lost ark". The presence of the German military seeking to recover artifacts of a religious secret [Holy Grail] was shown but with no background given the viewer on the issue. It was a fact that Hitler sent out his army to find the biblical [or suspected related] secrets of the ages.

Underlying the actions of Hitler was a belief in the lost city of Atlantis the sinking of which was, as he believed, due to the corrupt influence of inferior Jews. He believed that the Aryan [Nordic] race had been preserved only by fleeing to the heights of India from where they later returned to Europe. The Aryans were the blond blue eyed light skinned peoples of Europe and it was Hitler's plan to restore the primacy of the Aryan Race. [He apparently had no thoughts about other massive populations like Africans and Asians!]

Since Hitler did not believe in the resurrection of the human body as per Jesus Christ, his concept was one of reincarnation. That is the souls of those who die are reincarnated in a new body. His plan was to restore the supremacy of Aryan nations by killing off the mortal bodies of Jews and perhaps others whom he considered inferior to Aryan! He was sure that the souls of those inferior Jews would be re-incarnated in Aryan bodies and thus he would purify the earth from what he manically regarded as degenerate humans. Today we might think in terms of DNA.

His plan, The "Final Solution", would require that by death and/or sterilization he would ultimately remove what he madly considered to be an inferior race of people off the face of the earth! Hitler's plan was to use the political/military power of the state to achieve a religious goal. He was not alone in this. All those who belonged to the NAZI party had the same mindset. It was a plan based on racial genocide. In all of this, Hitler regarded himself to be a Christian which scholars have questioned. Had Hitler and Nazism [a form of religion] not been defeated, today, there would be a world without Jews and certainly no state of Israel!

It is also interesting that the Mormon Church supported Hitler in his early years as per an article appearing in the Church News published within the Deseret News on Dec.9, 1933. The article titled, **"Mormonism in the New Germany"** with a puff piece about Hitler and his entourage following the dietary code of the "Word of wisdom".

Additionally, it is evident that Hitler had studied the Mormon Faith to the point that he and his followers adopted the Mormon tradition of having "Fast" Sundays in which they abstained or fasted from eating and used the money saved to assist the poor. And the Mormon Church praised him and his followers for that practice. So much for the Prophet of God leading the Mormon Church!

It is argued by Mormon apologists that church leaders did not endorse Hitler but at the same time they did not condemn him! Some, but not all, Mormon Church leaders in Germany at the time were in fact Nazis!

At this point it is important to consider the similarities between Mormonism and Nazism.

*Total Dictatorship

*Corporate Black uniforms/suits of officers/ Elders.

*Brainwashed unthinking subservience of Subordinates

*Rapid discipline of dissidents

* Both "isms" were/are equally insane with parallel objectives to alter the nature and makeup of human beings, dead or alive

It has been recorded that American diplomats had criticized Hitler for his persecution of Jews. He retorted that the U.S. government had no room to speak since it had done the same thing with its treatment of Mormons.

The allegation of religious persecution was prominently used by the Mormon Church and it was mostly incorrect. Complaints of religious persecution were not centered on reality. There were stories of "Tarring and feathering" male members of the church. In fact my mother in her late teens in England was a witness to such an event. The Issue of polygamy in the later actions of the church became a handle for ridicule.

The more severe problems that the church had were related to an attempt to occupy the political scene and by sheer numbers, subdue opponents with assertions that the church was the only true church on earth restored by God through Joseph Smith, JR deserving political superiority. The "Saints" moved from location to location in groups and filled political areas en mass bringing fear to locals.

When that thinking hit a brick wall the only thing the church could do was to move to a new low population center and attempt to set themselves up again as the local political power. A population center where the local populace would submit to their overbearing claims of superiority.

It didn't work in Missouri. It did for only a while in Illinois until church founder Smith was killed and later it worked in Utah under Brigham Young until the Federal Government mistakenly thought it had brought it under control.

Americans and most Mormons today are unaware of the history so that when they look at Mitt Romney as the clean cut Presidential candidate with an attempt to make Mormonism just another "Christian" religion, the voter is duped and deceived into voting for him, a truly groomed Manchurian Candidate. [See Chapter 10 below] **The approach is the reverse of Hitler's this time; it is using religion as a disguise to politically conquer the world for God. Certainly a one world government as Hitler intended.**

Regardless of the method of conquest, it is all based on an insane delusion of religious fanatics who want to control the lives of the masses in order to seek some pleasing of a God they do not begin to understand. Or more so, the reality of gaining power and control over people, i.e. empire!

Christian Clergy while openly affirming that Mormonism is not Christianity fail to have studied in-depth the conspiracy of the Melchizedek Priesthood to seat it's "Prophet-King" as the secular head of world government similar to the quest of Adolf Hitler!

2

HOW ONE GETS BRAINWASHED

Brainwashing is defined as, "Subjecting a person to a prolonged process by which ideas other than and at variance to those already held are implanted in the mind." Being brainwashed is the condition of the mind after brainwashing.

However, not all brainwashed minds hold ideas that were originally held differently. This kind of condition is the result of having a prolonged concept of ideas tossed at a person from the beginning of life. Ideas which may be opposed to reality but nevertheless are ideas which a brainwashed person will literally give their life to live.

Hitler did it with his Hitler Youth. We saw examples of this in the Musical **Sound of Music**.

Since we are discussing Mormonism in this book let us talk about brainwashing Mormon style. Most all religions engage in the process.

For those who were unfortunate *[I say unfortunate because when and if the mind questions or challenges the order, doing so is a tremendous emotional challenge to overcome the years of in-depth brainwashing]* to be born into Mormonism because parents or a parent were/was a Mormon, brainwashing is a way of life. Shortly after birth the infant is held in the hands of Melchizedek Priesthood holders in the front of an LDS chapel and given a name and a blessing. Thus a commencement of lifetime brainwashing begins. If the father is a holder of the Melchizedek Priesthood, he usually performs the ritual with assistance from other "Elders". This Blessing constitutes membership in the church good for the first eight years of life. The innocence of a child to that age means that the child cannot sin. Only when the age of accountability is reached is there a need for baptism. Hence is it first a blessing not a Christening.

Parents are taught that if they fail to bring up the child in the church, they will be held responsible by God.

When the child turns eight years of age, he or she is taken into a baptismal font and submersed in water generally by a holder of the Melchizedek priesthood [however a Priest has authority to do the same] followed by a confirmation as a member of the church and given the gift of the"Holy Ghost" by laying on of hands of the lay priesthood.. All this is done in the presence of witnesses making the young believe in the sanctity of the ordinance.

Up to the age of twelve a girl and a boy are equal. After the age of twelve a distinct inequality begins. At age twelve, a boy is ordained a Deacon in the Aaronic Priesthood followed by ordination as a Teacher at age fourteen and then as a Priest at age sixteen. Both upgraded degrees of priesthood are within the Aaronic Priesthood. Since girls [women] may not hold Mormon priesthood, Aaronic or Melchizedek, they are inferior to males whom they give birth to as mothers.

During all this time from birth the child is exposed to the church with an encouragement that crying babies attend church with the mother in control even if the ward house [chapel] does not have a separated room with one-way glass where the general congregation is not subjected to the distraction of the child's noise but where the broadcast preaching of gospel is constantly tossed at the young mind through wall speakers.

Even when the child is out of the crying stage the preaching of the gospel is always being tossed at the child. Sunday school, Primary, Young People's Mutual Improvement Association Classes Boy Scouts and family home evenings. Under the plans of the church there is no escaping the mind's inundation of the peculiar religion.

Family home evenings are a weekly program of the church indulged in by Mormon families under direction of the priesthood holding father to further the indoctrination by brainwashing of the child in gospel subjects. The lessons taught are prepared by a special committee of the church and published yearly for distribution to families. Never is the opportunity for the child to consider to or listen to alternative ideas of the gospel. Nor is it allowed. Anyone attempting to teach alternative philosophies is speedily dealt with.

At age fourteen, the child of both sexes is conditioned by deeper indoctrination by early morning attendance at a church seminar located near a public high school. Again no consideration is given to alternative ideas. It is Mormonism in all its false **glory being incessantly dripped** into the impressionable mind of the child.

Traditionally the Catholic Church has said, "Give us the child; we will give you the adult". That is no different than the Mormon approach to teaching except the Mormon approach is more deliberate in penetrating the gospel illogically in the mind.

Being brainwashed after conversion to Mormonism is somewhat different due to the fact there is a mind with different ideas that have to be flushed out or rather suppressed by the educational program of the missionary system. This is more difficult since the new convert quickly learns that not all that was taught in the conversion process is true. This results in a large percent falling away or at least ceasing to be active in the church but with their membership still recorded on the records thus making the church appear to be larger than it really is.

Converts to the church only have themselves to blame for getting into the morass of Mormonism.

Many become "Jack" Mormons not attending but still in fear of speaking out against the church because they have learned there are "consequences" for such conduct.

At age nineteen or twenty the male member is expected to fulfill at least a two year mission around the globe to convert and baptize peoples to the church. Unfortunately for the church many missionaries come home from missions only to leave the church since their minds were broadened during the mission and the brainwashing gets washed away. Those are the lucky ones! I say this from my own experience and by interviews with those who have followed the light when a switch was turned on.

In my case it took many years after my mission, actually twenty years to develop the courage to be asking questions of those in upper echelons of leadership where the answers ought to be found. Actually the seed had been planted when I was only eight years of age but buried and forgotten for many, many years until a situation arose that triggered a recall. At that moment I moved from the doctrines of the church but with a sense of mission to expose what was wrong. This I would do in my own time and as conditions awakened me. But it was a daily struggle to stand against the years of brainwashing!

It is also significant that about eight percent of returned missionaries, males at least, have discovered they were homosexual and upon return are expected to follow a closeted life marrying and functioning as a "straight" male.

If exposed, they are dealt with severely as defects and pressure put on them to reconstitute their thinking. Many have committed suicide because they cannot live with themselves within the ignorant doctrines of church leaders.

3

HOW BRAINWASHING IS DEEPENED

The male member who becomes a missionary at nineteen or twenty or a female member who may wish to be a missionary are deepened into commitment to the church and thus to brainwashing by being required to obtain their endowments in a temple and to make solemn oaths prerequisite to the mission.

Members who do not go on missions are still expected at some time to obtain endowments in a temple. **Sworn secrecy to the temple ceremony is required and most faithful "brainwashed" Mormons honor that secrecy in spite of the fact that the ceremony is abundantly available verbatim in books and on the web.**

It becomes ludicrous to continue the secrecy in the face of such wide-spread public exposure. The church further brainwashes its members to a belief that it is sacred and thus requires secrecy. As a child I heard my parents say that every time they did a trip through the temple that they learned something new. Later in life I would realize that they would say this to justify a continuance in temple work trying to learn anything that they could to justify a lifelong indulgence in it.

In my own experience each time I attended I became more convinced that it was totally without merit and downright childish if not evil. Rather than referring to it as "sacred", I have thought of it as just plain stupid!

Another brainwashing of the temple ceremony is the wearing of secret and sacred underclothing which is supposed to protect the wearer against the assaults of Satan. However, they must be worn at all times-day and night even during sexual intercourse.

Being married in a Mormon temple or being sealed later in marriage is supposed to be for time and all eternity. By this method the church has learned to control the lives and finances of the patron who pay out ten per cent annually of their gross income before income taxes. In this day and age that could amount to an average of quarter million dollars lifetime per couple.

Probably unlike other churches, the LDS maintains detailed records of its members not the least of which is the payment of tithes into the church coffers. Based on those payments a person is granted or denied the right to go to the temple. A temple recommend must be held annually as proof of that right. Part of that approval is called "Tithing Settlement".

Repeated participation in baptizing for the dead and being "sealed" for the dead is another brainwashing of members the purpose being to keep the tithes coming into church coffers. Doing such work is referred to as being "saviors on Mt. Zion". In Chapter 14 I assert God will do away with the nonsense.

Baptizing the dead has included the Deist Founders of the United States as well as Adolph Hitler!

In time, Mormons will run out of dead candidates to baptize and grant priesthood rights to unless there is a large influx of the souls of persons killed by the so called Apocalypse.

However should the Priesthood succeed in capturing the governments of the world, the untimely deaths of adversaries is no problem as the records of the dead will be presented in the temples to have them "saved" by proxy regardless of race or ethnicity.

So Hitler killed Jews to have their souls re-incarnated as Aryans and Mormons would have the saved souls of the dead JEWS, NAZIS and all resurrected as Mormons.

Jewish groups are adamantly opposed to the church practice. Objections were made and promises of cessation made but not enforced.

4

HOW IT ALL GOT STARTED

The Joseph Smith, Jr. story has been told many times. I recall as a twenty year old missionary in the UK telling about young Smith in his fourteenth year [circa 1820] after being concerned about which church he should join, decided to retire to the woods behind his father's farm in Palmyra New York. As he knelt praying, a shaft of light descended from the heavens in which God the Father and His son Jesus Christ appeared. The Father pointing to the Son introduced Jesus as the beloved Son to whom Joseph should listen.

He was told all churches were an abomination and that in time he would be instrumental in restoring the true church to the earth. **At no point was there a reason or justification given for a belief in or need for membership in any church or even a need for "churches".**

Three years later began an annual series of experiences occurring during the time of the Autumn Equinox, September 21, 1823. He claimed to have had a visitation in his bedroom during the night by a resurrected angel "Moroni", who told him about some golden plates deposited in the earth on a nearby hill locally called, "Cumorah" near his home. On the plates was inscribed the history of a now partially extinct group of aboriginal people supposedly from the Palestine area.

He visited the site the next day in the company of "Moroni" and viewed the plates. Being told he would have to go through training and testing for loyalty for the next four years before the plates would come into his possession, he returned every year on the same day for four years. Finally on September 21, 1827 he claimed to have received them.

He told the story of his translating them with the help of glass lenses [seer stones] fixed in a metal bow called the Urim and Thumin [sort of like magic reading glasses]. The so called Egyptian hieroglyphs appeared as English words which Smith uttered and his scribe beyond the curtain would write down.

In early 1830, the book created from the translation known to this day as the Book of Mormon [BOM] was published followed by the organization of a church called the Church of Christ. That name latter changed to its present, the Church of Jesus Christ of Latter-day Saints. A more detailed history is available for those interested.

It turned out that the now official First Story preached by thousands of missionaries and by gospel teachers, this writer included, was in reverse. Only the story of the Angel Moroni and the golden plates was known by family, by neighbors and local townspeople and indeed through-out the missionary areas of activity for twelve years up until 1842 when Smith came up with the Father and Son First Vision. This was done to give more credibility to the sales and promotion of the BOM and the status of the church. There is no question but that historically the egg of Mormonism came after the chicken.

Enemies of the church have been quick to point out this discrepancy as proof on the conning nature of Smith while church apologists have been quick to retort that Smith considered the vision of the Father and Son to have been so sensitive to his work that it would be human nature to with-hold that information until such time as the work of the Book of Mormon was established before the real first vision could be brought out.

Today, in a little hamlet in Vermont called South Royalton, the Church maintains a visitor's center staffed by an elderly missionary couple who delight in telling the story of Joseph Smith Jr.

357 LDS Lane S. Royalton, Vermont 05068
Fair Use

Outside a granite tower stands 38 feet six inches tall representing one foot for each year of the life of Joseph Smith. Inside, a statute of Smith stands surrounded by couches for visitors to sit and gaze in awe at the replica of the man who, "communed with Jehovah".

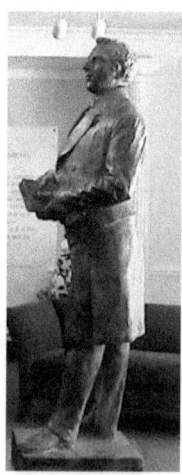

Fair Use

Not much happened here except it being the birthplace of Smith in December, 1805. For all practical purposes the life of Smith was spent in New York, Ohio, Pennsylvania, Missouri and Illinois where he died on June 27, 1844 at age 38 1/2 years under a hail of bullets from guns of his enemies. While some individuals were tried for the assassination no jury of non Mormons in the area would convict.

When I visited the visitor's center for the first time in early December 1998, about 193 years after Smith's birth, the elderly husband and wife visitor guides were augmented by an attorney, a Mormon, from a local community. What discussion I had with him was based upon his enthusiasm that should a current Gay rights Marriage law case pass in the courts of Vermont it would not take long to bring back polygamy in the LDS Church.

So despite the manifesto of church President Wilford Woodruff in October 1890, discontinuing polygamy, Mormon Males still have a phallic experience every time they contemplate a return to the practice of having several wives. Of course why would they not since the church has not stricken Doctrine and Covenants section 132's "New and Everlasting commandment" about polygamy from its scriptures? And why hasn't it? Simply because of patience. It has only suppressed and suspended it pending their gaining a political supremacy. See Chapter 26.

I served as a second counselor in a Bishopric in Portland, Oregon many years ago. At one point my fellow counselor asked me the question, "If the time ever comes that the church will be able to practice polygamy again and you were **lucky** enough to be selected to do it. How would you feel?" I told him he had answered his own question!

Polygamy as generally known is having plural wives on a concurrent horizontal time frame.

In this day and age vertical polygamy is practiced through divorce and remarriage. One could say the same for polyandry.

5

WHO THE HELL WAS

MELCHIZEDEK?

In Mormon Doctrine the first reference to Melchizedek is found in the book **Doctrines and Covenants** section 76:57 **"And are priests after the order of Melchizedek, which was after the order of Enoch. Which was after the order of the Only Begotten Son."**

The next is found in section 84: 14,15 the reference being that Abraham received his priesthood from Melchizedek and that the same was passed on down to Moses but was taken from the earth with Moses because God's people became too wicked to have it on the earth.

Moses' brother Aaron was given a lesser priesthood known as the Levitical [Both Moses and Aaron being of the tribe of Levi] or Aaronic priesthood after Aaron. That priesthood was passed down to John the Baptist who even baptized Jesus and later had his head cut off terminating that line of lesser priesthood upon the earth. Apparently there was only one holder of the Aaronic priesthood living at a time.

A study of Melchizedek shows that there is a tremendous amount of confusion as to his real identity. The prominent being that he was a righteous King of Salem at the time of Abraham. Some say he was Shem who would have been 450 years old when Abraham was 76. However we look at it, he was supposed to have been a high priest after the order of the only begotten Son of God i.e.: Jesus Christ. Of course Jesus was allegedly not born as the "only begotten" until some two thousand years after Abraham.

As such, the priesthood after the order of Jesus Christ (JC) had to have preceded Jesus on earth by Millenniums. Most scholars agree that the earth is by far older than the genealogy of the Old Testament and that at best Genesis is allegorical only and we cannot rely on it for historical truth or accuracy. Or for that matter, no record as to how Melchizedek acquired that priesthood or in fact that he ever existed! In Mormon thought it would be argued that God gave it to Adam and was passed on down to Shem or "Melchizedek" then to Abraham to Moses where it ended until such time as Jesus walked the earth and ordained his apostles who's followers [Catholics] went astray and was taken from the earth again

But according to Mormon scripture the Melchizedek priesthood authority was restored to the earth. In this regard Mormons believe in the pre-mortal existence of man and that Jesus Christ was the first born in the spirit world [but not the only begotten] and that whatever rights were given by father God to his first born in the flesh could be granted to worthy men in the flesh.

Since Joseph Smith, Jr. claimed to be a High Priest after the order of Melchizedek and further claimed to be the one and only who held all the keys to that priesthood who in fact gave authority to lesser holders of the priesthood for work they perform subject to his direction, we need to find out how he arrived at the conclusion he had it!

It is church doctrine that Joseph Smith, JR. has done more for the salvation of mankind than anyone save Jesus Christ.

6

HERE COMETH THE PRIESTHOOD!

Joseph had a helper in his translation of the "golden plates" into the Book of Mormon. Indeed his first helper was a gentleman farmer by the name of Martin Harris.

Under the procedure for the translation, Joseph would sit at one end of a table and Harris as scribe on the other end. Between them was strung a blanket or sheet so that neither of them could see the other at work. Joseph was variously spoken of as peering at the golden plates through a special device called the "Urim and Thumin" and at other times with his face buried in his hat. As he uttered the words he saw in English, the scribe would write them down on foolscap paper [Yellow legal paper].

This went on for some time until Harris argued he needed to take home some evidence to his wife that he wasn't just wasting time and squandering money on a foolish venture. As luck would have it, the papers were lost! Joseph after a time of delay with a new scribe, a school teacher named Oliver Cowdry returned to the work of translation but with the caution of not redoing the work that was lost. [This was in fear that the original may turn up later with an embarrassing different translation!]

At one point, questions about baptism came up and the two men retired to nearby woods to make further prayerful inquiry when all of a sudden the appearance of resurrected John the Baptist was present. He ordained them to his Aaronic priesthood. Being the Baptist the last holder of the Aaronic priesthood on the earth before his beheading now appeared as a resurrected being still possessing the office of the Aaronic priesthood. He put his hands on the heads of both Joseph and Oliver and ordained them as priests in that priesthood. Following that they retired to the nearby Susquehanna River to baptize each another.

This date May 15, 1829 was recorded by these men. As I recall they then each baptized one another and then ordained each other to that same priesthood with which they claimed possession of in order to have authority to baptize one another. This ceremony was supposedly recorded and the two men only had each other as witnesses to the event.

So when they came out of the river each was endowed with priesthood and had their lives cleansed by baptism. In the next chapter the name of Sidney Rigdon will be raised as a possible stand-in for the angel Moroni during Joseph's encounter with the angel. It has also been suggested that Rigdon was the "resurrected" John the Baptist who ordained these men.

Despite the careful reporting on the event and dating of the earth regaining a "legitimate priesthood authority" even though of minor authority, the reporting of the next step in obtaining the higher Melchizedek Priesthood was very sloppy.

"Sometime in the Month of June 1829", Peter, James and John the apostles of Christ,   appeared as resurrected beings to Smith and Cowdry and ordained them to the office of the higher priesthood. Huh? Again no witnesses; no details of where or exactly when this event happened and we are told to believe it!   There are literally a few million male members of the church who trace their priesthood to that ambiguous event.

The notion that such a powerful Melchizedek priesthood after the order of the Only Begotten Son of God was physically returned to the earth without any fanfare or explicitness in detail such as to a dating or location without any witnesses is a large swallow of faith in two men whose later actions in life belie their fidelity.

Before publishing the Book of Mormon [BOM] [A tangible product], Joseph required the witnessing of a total of eleven men [8 the first time and 3 the second] of the reappearance of the plates before he dared market the book in the world. But witnessing of the restored priesthood [faith only] needed none!

Yet the so-called witnessing event is flawed by reality. I will allow others to expose the psychology used by Smith in deluding the "witnesses". The fact that the whole enterprise in the beginning was financial in nature says a lot. The intent here is not to challenge the truth of the book but rather to expose the flawed use of the book and its history by the church in order to implement its future claim to be the physical political kingdom of god on earth with the leader of the church as "King". An issue which at the beginning of the national election year 2012 is of paramount concern for all Americans to realize what they are voting for in voting for Willard Mitt Romney for president

It must be remembered that the promotion of the BOM was initially a capitalist financial project without regard to it being promoted by a religious organization. Nothing Said here refers to the 4,000 plus+ changes made to the book after first publication.

It needs to also be remembered that the scheme of Smith and as later suggested, his cohort Sidney Rigdon, was to forever extinguish the actual existence of the "Gold Plates" by having the angel Moroni take them back into heaven or elsewhere so that no tangible proof of the plates exist whereby an educated translation could be undertaken to prove or disprove the Book of Mormon.

It requires a giant leap of faith to believe in the alleged original source of the BOM when the method of receiving, translating and hiding the source, i: e, the Golden plates smacks of elementary childish con artistry.

I would add that the genesis of the BOM* being so shadowy and flirting with dishonesty it takes literally an army of missionaries to convert relatively few converts annually.

The old saying, "You can fool some of the people all of the time and all people some of the time, but you cannot fool all the people all of the time.

*A study of DNA has proven the characters of the book having come to America from Jerusalem is a fraud. They came from Siberia.

7

BEWARE OF MEN SPEAKING AS IF THEY WERE GOD IN THE FIRST PERSON

Jesus we are told lived thirty three years on earth; the last three in his ministry yet not one word that he spoke was recorded during his life. All that we have are the sayings of Jesus that other men have written; men that never knew him in his own lifetime.

The first book, Mark, written about 67 AD was by a man that never knew him and never heard him speak. This was the first of the three synoptic gospels later followed by Mathew and Luke. These gospels are interdependent on each other with Matthew and Luke independently adding about 20-30 per cent each not found in Mark. None of these men knew Jesus or heard him speak. Whatever they could report was hearsay at best or fabrication at worst. Mathew and Luke pretty much mimicked the lead of Mark but with some variations. The Catholic Fathers were responsible for the arrangement of the gospels in the New Testament sequence of Mathew, Mark. Luke and John...

Well into the second century AD, John put forth his gospel and it was followed by Luke's Book of Acts which at best seemed to report the works of the apostles long after the death of Jesus.

None of these men knew either Jesus in the flesh or any of the apostles. Luke was not the same Luke as the apostle by that name. That being the case, the four gospels are unreliable and only allegorical. The words of Jesus came off the quill pens of the biographical writers or of their scribes. And of course translated into Elizabethan style by those who lived at the time of King James.

Joseph Smith, Jr. was prolific in speaking as if he were Jesus. Even the sections of the Doctrine and Covenant [D&C] quoted above were words of Smith as if he were Jesus. A clue to this is the prolific use of Elizabethan English throughout the so-called revelations Joseph claimed to receive from Christ. It was designed to give scripture sounding authority for the words when no authority existed.

Christ would have communicated as an American of Joseph's day and as if he had the general education that Joseph Smith would have used. Christ would not have spoken over the limited education of Joseph. It would have been more honest for Smith to have said, "And Jesus said to me".... Printing the D&C, the Book of Mormon or the book known as the Pearl of Great Price on fine biblical paper does not give scriptural authority.

The same argument applies to the excess Elizabethan style language of the Book of Mormon and also of the Pearl of Great Price containing the Books of Abraham and Moses which have been proven a fraud to everyone except the brainwashed followers of the false prophet Smith.

There are several thoughts on the origins of the Book of Mormon one of which is that it was written by a Dartmouth College graduate by the name of Solomon Spalding, the manuscript of which was later redacted by an early Convert and associate of Joseph named Sidney Rigdon; a defrocked Baptist minister who had enough biblical background to have inserted the Christian style doctrine into the manuscript making it what it became under Smiths, "translation". It has been suggested that at least two redactions were made.

A three volume study by Dr. William Whittsit donated to the library of Congress and now available on the internet in digitized format* suggests that Sidney Rigdon was the Angel Moroni because of his disappearances from his local community which coincided with the time frames of Joseph's reconnoitering with the Angel Moroni at the Hill

Cumorah on September 21, 1823, 1824, 1825, 1826 and 1827.

It is also interesting that a shirt tail relative of Joseph Smith by the name of Ethan Smith, also a Dartmouth graduate wrote a work titled, "A View of the Hebrews". It was a time when intellectuals were attempting to tie the history of the American Indians to a Jewish heritage.

In any event, the Book of Mormon has been disproven by DNA studies establishing that the Book of Mormon peoples came from Siberia not Jerusalem. This statement doesn't cover the fact that the book was privately corrected about four thousand times without the church leaders letting on.

We former Mormons, especially returned missionaries really regret that in our youth we allowed the church system to brainwash us into preaching the truth of the book when in fact there was none. It was written as fiction and today it so remains. If one can find any saving grace in it, it is only by metaphor to any moral principle that may have merit.

- ***Search for "Uncle Dale's" vast work on the internet.***

8

"THE LAW SHALL GO FORTH FROM ZION,

AND THE WORD OF THE LORD FROM JERUSALEM"

This somewhat abbreviated scriptural statement found at **Isaiah 2:3** reads: "For out of Zion shall go forth the law and the word of the Lord from Jerusalem". It was written presumably by OT prophet Isaiah prophesying of the future conditions upon the earth at the time of the commencement of the supposed thousand year reign of Shiloh when peace on earth is supposed to reign.

This statement is an extension of the patriarchal blessing given by Jacob (Israel) grandson of Abraham upon the head of Judah one of his twelve sons that later comprised the Twelve tribes of Israel. The blessing states that,"*The Scepter shall not depart from Judah nor the lawgiver from between his feet until Shiloh comes.*" Genesis 49:10 This has been interpreted to mean that the right of making law and governance of the political affairs of the world was given by God through Jacob to his son Judah and through his descendants until such time as the redeemer Shiloh is physically in control of earth's government.

Generally the Christian community considers Jesus to be Shiloh. First at the nativity and then secondly to appear just before the Millenium to reign through the thousand years of peace before the final end time.

The actual historicity or fulfillment of the Judah blessing proves otherwise yet there may be some tainting of the bloodline at various times and places in persons who held power of government, but certainly not exclusively. As such we can discount the promise as wishful thinking rather than a prophetic truth.

Mormon Founder Joseph Smith Jr. wrote up 13 articles of faith of his newly formed church. Article 10 states, **"We believe that Zion will be built upon this, the American Continent.......** He further elaborated that the Garden of Eden was located at Far West Missouri and that Zion would be established there. In other words, Zion will be built in Missouri, U.S.A. and the Mormon Church would be the kingdom of god on earth and that the prophet of the church would be the king of the kingdom.

Now Mormons consider themselves to be the elite of the earth. In fact Jews are considered by Mormons to be gentiles! However the Mormon church has patronized Israel to the point of dedicating the Palestine land for return of the Jews some 5 times between 1830 and 1948. Brigham Young University has an extension college there which can operate as a base for clandestine operations in Israel as against the Palestinian peoples much like the CIA out of U.S. Embassies.

The well known secret that Israel has multiple nuclear warheads* is a product of an unlawful gift by the Mormon Church [Melchizedek Priesthood] to Israel of Uranium mined in southern Utah during the early 1960's. More about that later.

*An Update [June 2012] would be that not only does Israel have nuclear warheads but also a navy with submarines armed with nuclear missiles.

9

ZION IN AMERICA

"Oye mountains high where the clear blue sky arches over the veil of the free! Where the pure breezes blow and the clear stream-lets flow how I long to your bosom to flee! Oh **Zion,** dear **Zion**, land of the free. Though thou wert (sic) forced to fly to thy chambers on high, yet we'll share joy and sorrow with thee." [Mormon Hymn, O Ye Mountains High, verse 2]

That verse is one of many LDS hymns I learned while raised as a Mormon in Utah and elsewhere. The hymn was written in Utah and bespeaks the praise of Mormons to the preservation of the church in what they considered the safety location goal of the church in the Utah Territory.

The name Zion has at least two connotations. The first is the name of the place in which God endows the government of the earth to his holy people. The second is of the pure in heart.

The hymn, as many others in the church song book, indicates the problem suffered by the church [body of people] in living the life that they have been taught to live under Joseph Smith's theocracy. It seems that everywhere the church escaped to, it ran into the problem of living in peace with its neighbors.

I recall as a child listening to my father relate the persecutions suffered by the early Mormon Church. While the church was organized in New York State its "persecution" really began in Ohio.

In Ohio, founder Smith picked up a convert counselor named Sidney Rigdon. Sidney Rigdon a defrocked Baptist minister [supra] was considered by Civil War Chaplain and Mormonism scholar Dr. William Whitsett to have provided Joseph with the story of the Book of Mormon contained in a dusty manuscript which he had discovered in a corner of a former bankrupt printing shop that had been written by a Solomon Spalding. Rigdon at the time was working in the print shop as he had lost his ministerial post.

After redacting the book to his personal Baptist philosophy he presented it to young Joseph over a period of time. Young Joseph had established himself with notoriety as a finder of buried treasure and was the target of Rigdon to present the manuscript. Rigdon knew that it would take some time to spring his fraud and he needed to prep Joseph to the task.

Rigdon's conversion after the church had been organized was a scam as he was in fact the true founder of Mormonism. The golden plates were in fact yellow foolscap paper on which Rigdon had made his second redaction of the Solomon manuscript.

In Ohio, Smith and Rigdon got in trouble with the law because they had organized a bank without state approval and were in fact selling securities on the bank for real money. They both fled to Missouri to escape criminal process in Ohio.

In Missouri, Rigdon at a fourth of July gathering in a park announced to the vast crowd that the church would "exterminate" the locals in order for the church to establish its Zion in America there. This resulted in Missouri Governor Boggs issuing an extermination order against the Mormons and a war called the Missouri War ensued. There were a number of skirmishes between state Militia and Mormons and the Mormons capitulated.

Joseph was given a military trial and was found guilty of sedition. He was ordered to be executed the next morning but after intervention by another Militia Officer that sentence was commuted to a civilian trial. Pending that trial he and co-defendants were housed in a jail known as Liberty Jail.

Liberty jail, Liberty, Missouri
Picture Public Domain

After several court hearings and changed venues Smith and his co-defendants were allowed to escape on horseback.

Previously, under terms of capitulation, the main body of Mormons had moved east to land across the Mississippi River which later was named Nauvoo, Illinois.

When Smith escaped he found his way to Nauvoo. There he became the big cheese again. He acquired a Masonic franchise and made himself a 33rd degree Mason "borrowing" rituals for use in the temple he was building. The franchise was forfeited because of that action.

Nauvoo was operated as a theocracy with Smith as mayor as well as the prophet of the church and Lt. General of the armed Nauvoo Legion.

Picture Public Domain

When word leaked out that a local newspaper, the Nauvoo Expositor, was about to publish an article concerning Smith's sexual affair with a 16 year old girl living in the Smith home, he ordered the press smashed.

About that time the State of Missouri sent over to Illinois a request for Smith's extradition as a fugitive from justice in Missouri. Actually Missouri was pleased to be rid of the Mormons however Governor Boggs had been the target for assassination by Joseph's body guard, Orin Porter Rockwell, and angered by that attempt decided to bring Joseph back for trial.

For smashing the newspaper press and the extradition request he was arrested and lodged in the Carthage, Illinois jail. In the late evening of June 27, 1844 Smith was shot dead by an angered mob.

Carthage Jail 1856

*Smith jumped out the second story window
exclaiming, "Oh Lord My God"
where his assassins shot him dead.*

Prior to that time in April 1844, Smith had announced his candidacy for US President after organizing the Council of the "YTFIF" [Fifty] which crowned him king of the earth. The purpose for organizing the council was for it to prepare the way for his election and for establishing the kingdom of god on earth with Smith as earth "King".

By 1846 matters had gotten so bad in Nauvoo, Brigham Young, as Smith's successor began a trek of the saints to Utah [Lands of the Ute Indians] or what at that time was a part of Mexico. By the time the "Saints" had arrived there the Mexican War yielded the area to the US and it was named the Utah Federal Territory.

Young as Prophet, Seer and Revelator became the political leader and was designated Territorial governor until the Utah War of 1857 when President Buchanan dispatched Johnston's army to quell an alleged rebellion against the Federal government.

At the time, there was no federal territorial law banning polygamy. In time, a territorial law of monogamy was passed by the congress thus outlawing polygamy. A case, Reynolds v. US (1878) did in fact affirm monogamy as the cultural persuasions of Western nations thus outlawing polygamy and the church was forced to officially abandon [suspend] it. The same thing happened to the Zion quest for empire of the church. They merely suspended it until such time as it would be opportune to revive it.

There has never been a time when the church has admitted what it was doing was wrong. It still intends to establish Zion by infiltration into agencies of the government not only the FBI and the CIA.

In addition, the church through its agents in government has been currently [2012] successful in locating the construction of a massive National Security Agency [NSA] facility in Utah which the church will be able to use it to suppress any opposition to its planned coup to take over the government of the United States. See www.american-united-against-fascist-and-theocratic-governmnet.org_ [also see chapters 20 and 21 below].

The church, since the time it arranged for Israel to obtain uranium mined in Utah in the 1960's, has had its own international spy system in operation using lapel pins as covert microphones and satellites to send stolen intelligence to Church tower storage computers in Salt Lake City. The pins came in three sizes and were under the control of the church public Relations officers.

Mormon Microwave Cavity resonator spy lapel pins
based on Russian KGB inventor Léon Theremin technology

The 2012 campaign for president has Mormon Mitt Romney among the candidates. As this is written, The Nevada caucus is ongoing and Romney is thought to out shine the other candidates.

Recently Romney took the lead in the Florida Primary and is favored to be the Republican candidate to face off with incumbent Barack Obama in the 2012 November elections.

Based on my childhood experience Mitt Romney, perhaps ignorantly, is an enemy of God!

10

MITT ROMNEY AS MORMON/MANCHURIAN CANDIDATE FOR PRESIDENT

Perhaps not all of us remember the movie "The Manchurian Candidate" a 1962 film. Adapted from a 1959 novel. The following is from Wikipedia, the free internet encyclopedia.

"Captain Bennett Marco, Sergeant Raymond Shaw, and the rest of their infantry platoon are kidnapped during the Korean War in 1952. They are taken to Manchuria, and are brainwashed to believe that Shaw saved their lives in combat — for which Congress awards him the Medal of Honor.

Years after the war, Marco, now back in the United States working as intelligence officer, begins suffering the recurring nightmare of Shaw murdering two of his comrades, all while clinically observed by Chinese and Russian intelligence officials. When Marco learns that another soldier from the platoon also has been suffering the same nightmare, he sets to uncovering the mystery and its meaning.

It is revealed that the Communists have been using Shaw as a sleeper agent, a guiltless assassin subconsciously activated by seeing the "Queen of Diamonds" playing card while playing solitaire. Provoked by the appearance of the card, he obeys orders which he then forgets. Shaw's KGB handler is his domineering mother Eleanor, a ruthless power broker working with the Communists to execute a "palace coup d'état" to quietly overthrow the U.S. government, with her husband, McCarthy-esque Senator Johnny Iselin, as a puppet dictator."

The novel has been adapted twice into a feature film by the same title, in 1962 and again in 2004. The 1962 film was based on the Korean War and the 2004 film was adapted to the gulf war. The plot in both of the films had to do with brainwashing. The first by the Communist in Manchuria and the second by an American Military industrial Corporation. The purpose was to pull off a palace coup d'état without violence by the voting process. The 2004 film is more in point to this writing, the 2012 election year!

How Does Mitt Romney fit into this article? Simply by the fact that he is a brainwashed High Priest of the Melchizedek Priesthood. The entity that created and controls the Church of Jesus Christ of Latter day Saints [LDS] or more commonly known as the Mormons.

As stated above, the Brainwashing of Romney is a standard practice of the Mormon Church. But he has been groomed to accomplish what his father George was not able to do back in 1967 when he ran for president.

With Mitt Romney's years in the church there is no question he is deeply brainwashed to the Mormon quest for empire to pull off a "palace coup d'état" That is to say that while he is boasting of doing good for America, his allegiance to the United States is secondary to his blood-oath sworn temple commitments to follow whatever the Church leaders ask him to do. What the church leaders are looking for is allowing them to become the de-facto presidency of the United States with Romney as their puppet.

Why would they do that? Simply because they believe as brain washed Mormons themselves that the church as it is constituted is literally the Kingdom of God on Earth with the church president as crowned earth king.

This allegation is proven by the actions of the church.

In 1959 one of their own wrote a book outlining church doctrine. While the printed beliefs of the church were framed in such things as the thirteen articles of faith only article ten gave a glimpse into the unpublished goal of the church. So for most Mormons in 1959 it was great to be able to read the doctrines of the church from A to Z in the book MORMON DOCTRINE by Bruce McConkie.

B

Book Cover 1966 Edition

Some members of the upper church hierarchy took issue with McConkie over some of his statements. As a result McConkie met with those leaders and edited the book which was republished in 1966. The book was again republished in 1979 to address the no longer credible statements about male Members of African origins since they were now able to hold priesthood based on the 1978 policy eradication of racial prohibition.

Mitt Romney ran for president in 2007 but dropped out after the religious issue of the "Mormon King" thing was raised. Embarrassed that someone actually had notice of that doctrine he had no satisfactory answer and dropped out. Subsequently John McCain took the GOP nomination but lost to Democrat Barack Obama.

In early 2010 about a year after the inauguration of Obama, the church quietly removed Mormon Doctrine from its Deseret Books store shelves and also saw to it that no more books were to be published. Under the circumstances of the church support of the Manchurian Candidate Romney running again in 20011/12 the church wanted to have deniability that it had any intention of pulling off a coup d'état in America with Romney's candidacy. The deniability would be that the book did not truly represent the goals of the church and that the church had no intention of seeking empire. The church was preparing for its coup d'état.

The following is taken from the 1966 book and is also in the 1979 edition.

Kingdom of God:

"The Church of Jesus Christ of Latter-day Saints (Mormon or LDS) as it is now constituted is the kingdom of God on earth; nothing more needs to be done to establish the kingdom. The Church and kingdom are one and the same." Pg 415

"The Church or kingdom is not a democracy; legislation is not enacted by the body of people comprising the organization; they do not make the laws governing themselves. The Church is a kingdom, The Lord Jesus Christ is the Eternal King and the President of the Church, the mouthpiece of God on earth, is the earthly king. All things come to the Church from the King of the kingdom in heaven through the king of the kingdom on earth". pg 416

"There is of course, the democratic principle of common consent where-under the people may accept or reject what the Lord offers to them. Acceptance brings salvation; rejection leads to damnation." Pg 416

"During the millennium, the kingdom of God will continue on earth, but in that day it will be both an ecclesiastical and a political kingdom. That is the Church (which is the kingdom) will have the rule and government of the world given to it. When inspired teachers speak of the future setting up of the kingdom of God on earth, they have reference to the millennial day when the "The kingdoms of this world are become the kingdoms of our Lord and his Christ; and he shall reign forever and forever."(Rev. 11:15)

"Daniel also saw the day when *the saints of the most High* (*LDS, added*) shall <u>*take and possess*</u> *the kingdom forever and ever.*" (Dan 7:18, 22, 27.) The Prophet (Joseph Smith) prayed that the present ecclesiastical kingdom of God on earth might roll forth that the future political and kingdom of God on earth might come". (Doctrine and Covenants (D&C) 65; Doctrines of Salvation, Vol. 1 pp 229-246.) pg 416

The attempt to take and possess the government of the United States is real. I taught it as a Mormon instructor many years ago. It is the ultimate goal of the church even if it borders on the crime of sedition.

So the church is attempting to block and discredit any current discussion of the issue. Deception is the hallmark of Mormonism from day one!

The removal of the book from church public sales was done with absolute secrecy. Fortunately the public was alerted to this by the effort of a local Salt Lake City Television Channel KUTV2. Otherwise we would not know about it.

So America, Nominate and elect Manchurian Candidate Mitt Romney as president at your own peril. Caveat Emptor "Buyer Beware".

11

WHAT TO EXPECT IF ROMNEY IS ELECTED

There is no argument that the United States military is the largest in the world and that expenditures to support it equals; or exceeds all the expenditures in total by all other nations combined.

It is also true that since President Polk ordered a false flag operation to justify an invasion of Mexico to steal [an armed robbery] the portions of ten western states to make the US a nation from the Atlantic to the Pacific. Quest for empire has been an active part of the government. No provisions in the Constitution allow that quest and mainstream Americans have no such agenda. It is an agenda of the elite who feel animal superiority over the rest of earth's inhabitants.

Since the Mormon Church has effectively armed Israel with nuclear weapons [chapter 22 infra] and the U.S. government has granted billions of dollars to Israel for its military technical supremacy in the area, you can be sure that a Romney/Mormon white house will join Israel in a war against Iran or any other Muslim nation that threatens the security of Israel.

A Romney White House and cabinet will be flooded with Mormon staff more than any previous administration and indeed the military will see Mormons promoted in rank to supervise all aspects of the military.

It will indeed be a time when every effort will be made to accomplish the goals preparatory to the prophesied "second" coming all for the glory of god!

Since the Melchizedek Priesthood does not believe in democracy, you may expect that the US Supreme Court will be suspended or modified to rule on theocratic issues according to the LDS Handbook of instructions as relates to the conduct of any member of the now existing Kingdom of God and further the Congress, if it is allowed continued existence, it will be a mere rubber stamp of the Melchizedek "king" who today is THOMAS STERLING MONSON.

Any persons seeking to confront the government about its goals will be swept aside, arrested and confined in military prisons [already in place] without any review under laws [**NDAA**] recently put in place by an ill witted congress and the spying of the Mormon controlled Utah Based NSA. Indeed the fears of Senator Frank Church will be present [See chapters 19-20 below].

Theocratic [fascist/Communist] rule will include the forfeiture of the assets of everything owned by the peoples of the kingdom in accordance with the suspended, "United Order" of LDS founder Joseph Smith where the kingdom owns everything and dispenses according to its determination of need.

For more aggressive "patriots" the Mormon backed Garden Plot* conspiracy of the 1950's will be unleashed and indeed many persons unsupportive of the government will be shot and buried [disappeared] without seeing a lawyer or a court room. This will be implementation of the King Laban Doctrine of the Book of Mormon in which justified murder is used to save the continuity of the kingdom and the soul of the victim(s) under the Blood Atonement doctrine [justified murder].

The obedient mentality of former Nazi heel-clicking arrogance, normally abundant in the Mormon Melchizedek Priesthood, will rampage across America by martial law.

Nations that refuse to fall into line will be obliterated or subdued by military threat. Romney will be following the mentality of his priesthood superiors or he too will be swept aside and his authority usurped by the Mormon Prophet. In other words, Mormon control of America's military and its 600 plus military bases around the world will result in a quick and sudden manner to prepare the entire world by death and devastation for the millennial reign of Christ's man on earth in charge, the "Mormon king, i.e. the Mormon Prophet.

The pattern [Bush Doctrine] of if you are not with us you are against us and therefore subject to extinguishment will prevail over America and the world. It will the darkest period of history ever known to the world and indeed could spell the end of it!

The history of the Mormon Church in dealing with dissidents or its enemies has never resulted in conciliation or compromise. Suspension yes but never conciliation! It is their way or the highway. In fact the horrors of the Third Reich will be revisited. Democracy will be replaced with Fascist Theocracy and there will be no tolerance for non-support.

Can't happen in America you may say? The 1917 Bolshevik revolution swept communists to power in Russia. "Bolshevik" is a term for a minority. The Bolsheviks comprised no more than two percent of Russians yet they were able to set up the conditions for the revolution and for its success.

There has been no total numbers reported of the people who were assassinated or placed in camps in Russia under Stalin or his predecessor, Lenin. We know they are in the millions.

Hitler's Third Reich was responsible for the deaths of sixteen million. In fact any time you establish a closed society that does not allow for dissention and transparency there will be a corresponding reduction in population and/or an increase in illegal incarcerations.

Brigham Young's Utah had its night riders led by gunslinger Orin Porter Rockwell who kept the populace in place and overtly supportive of Young. Those that caused dissention were "backlotted", [inspiration for 1950's "Garden Plot"?] that is killed and buried in their back yards.

The evil of the 1857 Mountain Meadows Massacre in Southern Utah [September Dawn] was carried out by devout Mormon Priesthood holders following orders of their superiors killing, in cold blood, about 120 men, women, teenagers and children down to the age of 3 or 4. Two men escaping from the group on foot the night before were tracked down by men on horseback and their throats slashed. Even though participants like John Doyle Lee** wept while the massacre was ongoing, he did nothing to stop it as it was a **Melchizedek Priesthood Operation from**

top to bottom. They did it before and they can do it again!

Today, Mormons comprise about 2% of the population and are quite capable of pulling off a coup similar to that of Lenin and the Bolsheviks. It will be done without violence in the beginning. Just good looks and family values will deceive American voters into buying the fascist theocratic dictatorship. Once in they will be impossible to get rid of because of the intelligence obtained from the controlled **NSA DATA CENTER** in Utah. It is better to avoid the deception than to ignorantly buy into it.

An old expression [PERHAPS JOKINGLY] about converting peoples of the world to the Mormon doctrine is made easier after they are dead.

Doing the Temple saving ordinances of proxy baptism and priesthood ordination is very simple and Mormons will have met their obligations of being "saviors" on Mt Zion. Since salvation and exhalation in the never ending afterlife is of far more importance to the church leaders than living on the fringe of hellish mortality. Killing resistors and doing their temple saving baptism would be justified* and surely drone aircraft killings and remote operations are less personal and easier to execute.

Using powers claimed to be from God and temples as "holy" sanctuaries to convert the

spirits of the dead from what they died as into Mormons would be justified by the "Kingdom of God on Earth"!

Doesn't that sound like Hitler's modus operandi of making Jews into Aryans?

LDS Church World Headquarters 50 East North Temple Salt Lake City, Utah. The church is established in 160 Countries of the world.

Garden plot was investigated by US Army Intelligence in the 1950s and led to the doors of the Mormon Church, yet nothing was done about it.

**Lee's was the only prosecution, conviction and execution of the purely Melchizedek Priesthood massacre Operation. Native Indians said he was the man who cried during the killings.

12

A vote for Mitt Romney is a vote for the Mormon Prophet-King!

"...If the Constitution be saved at all it will be by the Elders of this Church"

During Joseph Smith's lifetime he is claimed to have made a hearsay statement that the time would come when the Constitution of the United States would hang, "as if by a thread" and if it be saved at all it would be by the elders of the [this] church. That statement is known by literally every priesthood holder in the United States and in foreign nations.

This statement followed a dissertation about God having raised up the Founding Fathers to create a god inspired constitution the most perfect in all history.

Every Elder is anxiously awaiting the day when they can step in under the "Prophet's" direction and participate in saving the Constitution. When I was younger and an active priesthood elder I was very much aware of this claim or statement allegedly made by Joseph Smith, JR.

In my thinking, the saving of the constitution had to do with an honest effort to preserve it as against the efforts of those who would change our democratic republic to a fascist or theocratic dictatorship. I thought that to be a noble undertaking by Mormon Elders. As a gospel instructor I taught it.

Along with the idea of saving the Constitution is the doctrine of the Mormon Church becoming the secular earth government. This I also taught.

Upon examination, the two ideas are opposed. On the one hand is a democratic republic with a notion of citizen participation. On the other is the notion of a religious dictatorship. Indeed I never fully analyzed that disparity.

My first viable encounter of notice with the "saving" notion was in the mid 1960s. A rumor had circulated during the early morning priesthood meeting [in the (tenth Ward) sharing the Mount Tabor Chapel, Portland, OR] that the church had invented a device to help it save the constitution. I didn't take much notice but a few years later discovered the church had indeed acquired a device that would be worn on the lapels of elders whenever they wanted to gain intelligence on some target. It would be put into operation when the Church Tower on North Temple [SLC] was completed.

A fellow elder had given me more info and I declared it to be a diabolical plan to invade privacy. That was my first learning that **subterfuge** would be used by the church in order to, "save the constitution."

I told my friend if I ever saw it in action I would expose it. Fear filled his eyes and he said," You wouldn't", I assured him I would and I did. See my memoirs.

The notion of saving the Constitution is a ruse that will allow the church to pull of its coup for conquest of empire!

In my Memoirs I talk about being hired by the church in January of 1951 right after my mission to work in the building department then housed on the 4th floor of the church office building at 47 E South Temple street Salt Lake City [SLC]. I also talk about visiting my former boss, Julian Cannon, some twenty years later. At that time, the long planned church tower at 50 East North Temple was nearing completion. During the discussion about the tower he informed me that the top four floors would be completed after he was forced to retire and he had not seen any interior finishing plans.

When I asked him what those floors would be used for his reply was, "Beats the hell out of me. All I know is they are building it like a fort"!

In Under the Mormon Tree I discuss the several times the technology was used against me in the run-up to my ordaining a Black man between May 1975 and April 1976. I have noted on the website, Americans United..., that the US government via NSA is building a very large storage facility for stolen intelligence 26 miles south of Salt Lake City. That facility will be used by the church to pull off its coup under pretense of saving the Constitution.

The NSA facility under construction in Utah
26 miles south of SLC. FAIR USE

A part of the successful ruse to acquire the presence of the facility in Utah is the overt patriotism of Mormons employed by the government and the ability to use the missionaries of the church as quasi intelligence agents to gather the sought after information in the phony war on terrorism.

It has been a fact that in the past at least, returned Mormon missionaries were hired without any testing as required of non-Mormon applicants. The fact of knowledge of a foreign language skill together with their patriotism being the attraction.

In past times Ezra Taft Benson and Reuben J. Clarke [after whom the BYU Law School is named] were members of the executive Branch of government.

At the present time, Both the Congress and the Department of Defense have established laws and conditions to make it ripe for pulling off the takeover of the US government destroying freedom and replacing it with a Nazi style fascist dictatorship.

How many Mormons in government have been conspiring to achieve this can only be guessed. We do know that Senator Orin Hatch was at the ground breaking ceremonies in January 2011.

So the facility will be complete with electronic eavesdropping from the entire world wired into the Utah Data Center for use by the Mormon King Thomas Sterling Monson. This is an issue which needs the full attention of the government **NOW!**

Photo: Name Withheld; Digital Manipulation: Jesse Lenz

UTAH DATA CENTER UNDER CONSTRUCTION EVEN AT NIGHT
HURRY UP! WE NEED IT FOR MITT ROMNEY'S PRESIDENCY!

PART TWO

THE FOLLOWING IS A COLLECTION OF ESSAYS OF THE AUTHOR RE-INFORCING THE ASSERTIONS OF THIS BOOK. THERE WILL BE SOME REPITITION OF POINTS ALREADY MADE

Additional essays can be read and downloaded from Opednews.com and NowPublic.com

In any event there is an expose' of the nutty-ness of Mormon doctrine which disqualifies the Melchizedek Priesthood from politically controlling planet earth.

13

MORMON CHURCH

LEADERS LIE!

In the winter of 1992, a documentary film made by Jeremiah Films began distribution. The video, "GODMAKERS II" contained a 3 minute segment which alleged Mormon Church president Gordon B. Hinckley had a past life of kinky sex after he became an Apostle of the church. The film alleged homosexual activity on the part of Hinckley as well as sex with both black and white prostitutes and young boys.

The church quickly countered with a notice to its members worldwide that the allegations of the film had been investigated by an independent non-Mormon attorney and were proven false. The church notice went on to say that the testimonies of people speaking in the video had been recanted.

After the notice had been publicized, a Salt Lake City attorney,* a non-Mormon, wrote a letter to the filmmakers intending to intimidate them with veiled threats of a lawsuit if they did not withdraw the video from distribution.

Doug Wallace, a Washington State attorney, answered that letter. Wallace had been instrumental many years earlier in persuading the Mormon Leaders to abandon their policy of race discrimination against Blacks. He had ordained a Black a priest in a Portland, Oregon Motel swimming pool in 1976 and even though "excommunicated" from the church for that act, kept pressure against the church. Finally in 1978, church president Spencer Wooley Kimball had a "revelation" which allowed for Black men to hold priesthood.

Responding to the church attorney, Wallace demanded proof that he was indeed retained by the church to attempt intimidation of the filmmakers. He produced a letter over the signatures of the two counselors of Hinckley in the First Presidency of the church.

Wallace attempted to have the attorney point out what items or areas of the GODMAKERS II video were false. The attorney never made any statement of any specific part of the video to be false. The attorney attempted to persuade Wallace that the statements made by individuals on camera in GODMAKERS II had been recanted but was never able to specifically state which of the individuals had recanted or when they had recanted.

Wallace almost begged the attorney to file a lawsuit against the filmmakers with a statement, "Truth, as a defense, will bury you and your clients." The attorney backed off and no lawsuit was ever filed.

The church notice to members remains a deliberate lie.

Ask any church member today and they will repeat the lie told them by church leaders in early 1993, that an independent attorney investigated and reported no truth in the video and a recanting of statements made. The church member today relies on the bogus statement as truth.

Meanwhile, GODMAKERS II video continues to enjoy wide distribution. That video is available through Jeremiah Films of Hemet California. Orders@jeremiahfilms.com

- The author is with-holding the name of the attorney

14

MORMON QUEST FOR EMPIRE: GOD'S TAKE ON IT AND THE 1937 "GOD, I KNOW YOU ARE IN THERE!" EPISODE

As a child in Ogden, Utah on May 8, 1937 which also happened to be my 8th birthday, I Shouted at God while looking at the Mormon Eighth ward chapel a block east of Washington Blvd. on the corner of Seventh street, "**God, I know you are in there!**" I will hereafter refer to that event as the, "**EVENT**"

The occasion for that outburst was that some of my close church/school buddies had just been kicking my butt for implicating them a couple of weeks earlier in a strawberry cup burning episode in the back yard of one of our neighbors and I was laying my hurt on God.

Shucks, it was my birthday and I had a bicycle albeit an old used adult three wheeler that my dad had dug a basement by hand to acquire. It was depression time and while he was a skilled carpenter-contractor from the old country [UK] he took whatever work he could get to feed his large Mormon family of six children. A part of his pay had been that old bicycle.

Actually in those tough times, that gift made me the only kid on the street that had "wheels" and I mistakenly thought I could plaster over the ill feelings by sharing those wheels with my buddies. What a mistake! It seemed that after the cops had visited their parents with my story about the berry cup burning affair and their denials of complicity, they had been told not to associate with me. Later of course that smoothed out.

In my memoirs, *UNDER THE MORMON TREE,* I explain all about that episode. I do also explain what happened immediately following that oral outburst directed to God. The event was what is often called an epiphany. That is I experienced a contact from the unseen world. You know the world that people refer to as "heaven" or the "spirit world" which they are sure exists but never see until dead...that is if they are lucky. I say lucky because experiences like that can really screw up a person's life. I know because I have been there and witnessed that!

You see its okay if old fogies of a couple of thousand years ago had or faked similar experiences which they used to build a faith based religious system creating many world churches. But not these days for God doesn't talk to man anymore as his word is written in the Bible! Yet we are taught to pray to God for help and we do it by the thousands and millions. I often wonder what would happen if God occasionally appeared in public and gave a response to the prayers of those millions. I guess no one would accept it unless God were illuminated with heavenly shafts of light and surrounded in the clouds with thousands of angels and seen by many people.

For the most part, people who have had such experiences are very reluctant to talk about it for fear they will be put in a locked straitjacket and trucked off to the nut farm or be avoided like the plague. So the usual practice is to keep it inside and never tell a soul. And I "gotta" admit that is what I did...for many years. People who have never had an epiphany disbelieve those who have.

Some hundred and eight years before my birth a young man claimed he had a vision of God and Jesus before or after having an angel lead him to gold plates buried in a small hill in New York State so that he could bring forth a new bible and a new religion known as Mormonism. That guy was known as Joseph Smith JR. The combined story is historically conflicted and is a classic, "which came first the chicken or the egg" question.

Today he has followers supposedly in the 12 or 13 millions around the globe. Indeed one of those members named Willard Mitt Romney with the support and backing of the Mormon leaders and church members is gearing up for his second attempt to be elected president of the United States. Unfortunately for me that is where the, **"EVENT"** comes into play.

Being born in Utah, the Mormon Bee Hive state, was not a blessing for me unless I make a confession that the experience on May 8, 1937 destined me to spend another 76 plus years expecting to do or to avoid doing a work which was entrusted to me as a result of shouting at God in the **"EVENT"**

Of course I didn't really expect an answer. I had left the company of those buddies and was cycling down 7th street when I turned right at the Ogden eighth ward chapel to peddle my birthday bike around the Lincoln Elementary school yard [play ground] about three blocks north.

When I got there I had the experience of a lifetime. I found out that God doesn't dwell in structures made by the hand of man as I had thought. Yet that knowledge and what else I experienced would escape my memory and lay in the far reaches of my consciousness for many years. But what did stay within me those many years was a belief that I had seen and communicated with Jesus and I was given a job to do but I never let on. Not to friends, not to siblings, not to parents.

Figure 1
Lincoln Elementary school and playgrounds
where the "**EVENT**" happened May 8, 1937

Thirty Seven years later after a lifetime of service within the Mormon Church, in late summer, 1974, I had an opportunity to spend some time alone with my dad. He and mother had converted to Mormonism before any of us siblings were born. Indeed before they met and married in England during World War I.

The present scene was waiting in a motor home in the parking lot of the Oregon Caves in southern Oregon while Mother, my wife and our kids had gone down into the dark caves. Our four month old young son was sleeping in a crib and dad was slowly dying of heart failure.

Over the years I had told my dad of certain "spiritual" events in my life but without any hint of the 8th birthday "**EVENT**". **"Did all those things really happen to you?"** was his query to start off the conversation. "YES", was my response. Looking into dad's azure blue eyes made me truthful as nothing else could. He then said he believed me because I had never in my life lied to him. I assured him there was one time. After reviewing some experiences he expressed to me that his faith in me was such that whatever or where ever those "experiences" led me with regard to the church, I had his approval to follow them. That expression meant a lot to me.

Figure 2
Dad Wallace dressed as Joseph Smith, Jr.
In a pageant in the UK at time when he was
acquainted with Mitt Romney's
missionary Father, George.

Previous to that time I had been attempting for four years to flush out the thirty seven years old "**EVENT**" on the Ogden Elementary school ground. I was doing this in strict compliance with Mormon standards. As a High Priest in the North Columbia River Stake of the church, my priesthood senior was the Stake President, Wallace (Wally) Teuscher. I met with Wally several times and ultimately he gave me a letter of introduction to Spencer Kimball, president of the Council of the Twelve Apostles, in the hope of helping resolve my "dilemma" as he called it. Kimball was recuperating from open heart surgery and passed me off to another Apostle, LeGrand Richards. Richards had been my employer as Presiding Bishop of the church about twenty years earlier when I had just come home from a mission to the UK. Richards also had officiated at the Salt Lake Temple wedding ceremony of me and Patricia in January of 1953 a year after the mission. So I was glad to communicate with him but above all I sought a personal one on one communication.

The exchange of correspondence [which I still have] with Richards went nowhere as the purpose of this exchange was to have a personal one on one meeting with a member of the council of the twelve whom I would expect to be able to interpret the Lincoln Elementary school experience. After all these men were/are considered to be prophets in touch with God on a daily basis. Surely there could be no shaman on earth with superior credentials! I was denied that experience. I could have done just as well or maybe even better with a Gypsy palm reader. I did however begin to consider these men to be imposters misrepresenting themselves to their followers.

Spencer Kimball, when informed of the exchange wrote me and told me that if I ever had what I a **"thought was a revelation, to merely lock it in my heart and never tell a soul!"** he also asked me to drop him a little "note" and tell him I would comply which I never did. Within a few years he would become President/Prophet of the church. We did meet briefly once.

Somewhat later, February 1974, I succeeded in having a meeting with Apostle Howard Hunter in the Columbia River Stake Center. However it was not a one on one* where the issues could be easily discussed. The meeting had two other lesser official church officers present with whom I did not want to discuss personal issues. However an urge came over me to ask Brother Hunter if he had ever seen the Lord? It is supposed the name"Apostle" means a personal witness for Christ. His reaction was to literally scream as he turned his head to the wall presumably in shame," **If I ever did, I would never tell a soul"!** He also told me that if I persisted in doing what I was [asking questions] I would be destroyed! So much for obtaining counsel from imposters. Now since I thought that I had seen Jesus myself all those years earlier, I was maybe one up on Hunter! I later learned that was wrong [later learned to be "Michael"] but not on the communication. At that time I was only seeking answers.

Still later, May. 1975 I had the opportunity to speak with the male secretary for the then church, "prophet, seer revelator/president, Spencer Kimball, a guy named D. Arthur Haycock who was the first to use the lapel pin spy technology on me. It would be used several times later.* this occurred after flying to Salt Lake City and meeting him in the outer office to Kimball. That was followed by a meeting with my old boss LeGrand Richards on an upper floor. His secretary was shaking as she directed me into his office and Richards was also shaking with old age or fear or both who asked me. "Why are you doing this? **Why are you not helping build up the Kingdom?"** I assured him I was not his enemy and he calmed down and we talked but to no advantage. He told me that Kimball the Prophet and seer had asked his advice about what to do with Israel?

As additional precursors, I met with W. Cleon Skousen the evening before speaking with Haycock and Richards and I had corresponded with Mitt Romney's father, George Romney, a past friend of my father in the UK both of these men were well known Mormons and they each told me to follow my own conscience.

In all, I spent about five years of my life attempting to decipher the May 8, 1937 **EVENT** with men whom if they were actually in touch with God could have helped me. It did appear as though they felt threatened thinking my quest was to replace them. Much later in August 1977 as reported in my memoirs, a court case was heard in the Third Judicial District Court in Salt Lake City and I was asked a question by the church attorney Alan Swan, "Do you want to be president of the church"? My answer was only long enough to clean up the mess it was in. He showed disgust on his face at such an answer.

However three months after my trip to Salt Lake city on August 17,1975 my dad passed away leading up to my determination to follow conscience and challenge the church leadership. That happened and I was led to take action to break the Black priesthood racism inequality nonsense which I did with an ordination of a Black man on April 2, 1976. What I did could likely have been prevented if the leadership really had the gifts and authority they espoused. But that was not in the cards despite the brainwashed beliefs of church followers.

The episode of the Lincoln Elementary experience unfolded to memory as I proceeded to follow hunches and premonitions after April 2, 1976. Doing the ordination was the key to opening the mystery of the "**EVENT**". In fact it began almost immediately.

Since I am attempting to publish this on Opednews.com, I need to jump ahead in this article as items that are on the fringes of human experience are not provable and therefore unsuitable for publication. For those who wish to read it I suggest going to page 139 of my memoirs Under the Mormon Tree where you can read it. If you don't have the book, email me and I will send you a PDF of chapter 22. Or, go to Nowpublic.com where it appears without the graphics. **http://my.nowpublic.com/culture/god-and-mormonism-another-view-short-title**

Gleaning information received from recall of the "**EVENT"** and putting it bluntly, the upshot from the recall of the epiphany which unfolded naturally to me after April 2, 1976 and is found on Pages 143 and 144 of **Under the Mormon Tree** are as follows:

- *God does not dwell in chapels, Cathedrals or Mormon Temples made by the hand of man. He only dwells in human beings that love and "know" Him.*

- *God expressly stated He will in time terminate the Mormon Temples and the folly that goes on within the temples, i.e. eternal marriage/sealing, endowments and salvation for the "dead".*

- *God considers the plot of the Mormon Church to build up the Kingdom of God on Earth with itself as the temporal kingdom in keeping with "prophecies" of Daniel to be another folly that will be ended.*

Reading between the lines of what I do now know from the 8 year old child **"EVENT"**, coupled with years of active church membership, a second epiphany before World War II and the learning of many scholars researched over the past several years, I feel we can further recognize God's mind regarding the following issues. Taking this all in I find myself standing philosophically in the company of George Washington, John Adams, Benjamin Franklin, Thomas Jefferson and other founding fathers who considered themselves to be Deists. According to that reasoning God rarely if ever interferes with conditions on the earth.

1. There was no mention of world religions other than the Mormon Church in the dialogue. And apparently God is not concerned about them because they are not mentioned. Why I do not know at this point. It likely could be that churches have no impact

positive or negative on the afterlife apart from spiritually gaining wisdom, taming the spirit and learning unconditional love in this life.

2. Priesthood** is a man made fabrication as God could not trust fallible mortals with authority to act in His name and further, there is nothing on this earth that requires the intervention of God except, as I am informed, the existing insane Mormon plot of gaining a world empire. It is academic that no one needs priesthood to do well unto others.

3. God is not otherwise concerned with the folly of mankind for all future life continuing after mortal death is naturally pre-planned for and accommodated by him without regard for churches.

4. God is not impacted by praise or honorariums or curses or atheist denials of his existence as he is secure and above it all.

The point is that the "**EVENT**" episode currently applies to Mitt Romney and/or any other Mormon from this point in time on. Only by repudiating all the nonsense of Mormonism which they have espoused or partaken of in the past shall they ever be allowed to be president of the United States. It might well be that when church leaders belatedly discover God's will in this they will back off their ego trip and dissolve the dogmas of Mormonism. However, admittedly, there would be nothing left to justify the existence of the church.

While the Constitution may prohibit a religious litmus test for candidates to public office, the fact that The Mormon Priesthood has a history of seeking an overthrow of democracy in order to implement their notion of a Kingdom of God on earth as diametrically opposed to the provisions of the Constitution it is therefore political and needs to be considered by rational people.

The evil of Mormonism in this day and its conspiracy to control the world is demonstrated in the following websites: www.americans-united-against-fascist-and-theocratic-government.org

www.underthemormontree.com

*The standard practice is to go two by two so that the one can ride herd on the other, i.e., as missionaries do.

** The issue of my ordaining Larry Lester to priesthood on April 2, 1976 was really an expression of equality of the races not that of gaining priesthood rights as such for there really aren't any!! Man may make himself a priest but God does not have to recognize it.

15

December 12, 2011

HOLY BLOOD, HOLY GRAIL AND THE DA VINCI CODE: IS ROMNEY THE FRUITION OF MORMON BELIEF THAT CHRIST WAS MARRIED MAKING ROMNEY HEIR TO EARTH KINGSHIP?

The following is borrowed from:

http://www.i4m.com/think/bible/mormon-jesus-married.htm

"The Scripture says that He, the Lord, came walking in the Temple, with His train; I do not know who they were, unless His wives and children."
- *The Prophet Brigham Young, Journal of Discourses Vol. 13, p.309*

"There are those in this audience who are descendants of the Lord's Twelve Apostles-and, shall I say it, yes, descendants of the Savior himself! His seed is represented in the body of these men."
- *LDS First Presidency Member and Apostle George Q. Cannon, Solemn Assembly in the Salt Lake*

Temple, July 2, 1899, Meeting Notes Utah State Historical Society, p. 376.

Mormon doctrine teaches that Jesus Christ was married also, but there's more...

Start by reading Mormon scripture D&C 113:1-6. According to the chapter heading, this Q&A revelation session was conducted by the Prophet Joseph Smith himself both as interrogator and the Lord...

1. Who is the Stem of Jesse spoken of in the 1st, 2d, 3d, 4th, and 5th verses of the 11th chapter of Isaiah?

2. Verily thus saith the Lord: **It is Christ.**

3. What is the rod spoken of in the first verse of the 11th chapter of Isaiah, **that should come of the Stem of Jesse**?

4. Behold, thus saith the Lord: It is a servant in the hands of Christ, who is **partly a descendant** of Jesse as well as of Ephraim, or of the house of Joseph, on whom there is laid much power.

5. What is the root of Jesse spoken of in the 10th verse of the 11th chapter?

6. **Behold, thus saith the Lord, it is a descendant of Jesse, as well as of Joseph, unto whom rightly belongs the priesthood, and the keys of the kingdom, for an ensign, and for the**

gathering of my people in the last days. (*See also D&C 110:16. In fact, most of D&C 110.*)

Is the hope of the future Mormon kingdom of god on earth hanging on the election of Mitt Romney?

During my active years as a Mormon, I taught adult gospel doctrine classes as well as both adult Aaronic priesthood classes and Elder's Quorum classes. In fact I was known in the Pacific Northwest as a "Gospel Doctrinarian" and answered calls from church members from around that geographic area.

The beliefs of the church which can be publicly presented are set forth in a statement or creed known as the 13 Articles of faith.

Other beliefs and practices of the church which cannot be publically presented are such things as Temple ceremonies; blood oaths and blood atonement, commitments of obedience and consecration of all one's possessions to church leaders if requested and the existence of the obedience enforcement side of church starting with Bishops and Stake Presidents,

Excommunication councils followed up with sinister image protection agents who are privately hired to plot, plan and execute operations against former members or non members who have cast a pall of discredit over the church and it's covert acts of financial and political intrigue.

Dictionaries name these individuals as "Danites". They also fall within the area of planning and intrigue of what was originally created by founder Joseph Smith, JR as the Council of the "YTFIF" or FIFTY. It was that organization that actually did the work and planning for the pioneer trek from Illinois to the Salt Lake Valley. Brigham Young has been given the credit for planning the trek but it was the effort and skill of those men who brought the success to the effort.

Quietly spoken by the priesthood of the church is the belief that Jesus Christ was a polygamist having several wives and numerous children who survived him. This belief is not based on public doctrine yet it falls into place as an unofficial doctrine as noted in the beginning paragraphs of this article.

The book, **Holy blood, Holy Grail** suggests a belief that Christ did not actually die on the cross but that he survived and that his descendants traveled to southern France and later dispersed to other locations. The Holy Grail could likely be proof of kingly right [Rex Deus] descendants one of whom would arise in the latter days with the right and authority to head the Kingdom of God on earth.

The book, **Rosslyn: Guardian of the Secrets of the Holy Grail** by Tim Wallace Murphy & Marilyn Hopkins suggests that Rosslyn Chapel in Scotland hides the proof laid there by the Knights Templar that indeed a blood line from Jesus exists to this day.

With its well known prowess to research genealogical records from around the world, it would likely be a credible attribute of the Mormon Church to come up with a pedigree chart showing that indeed **Willard Mitt Romney is a literal descendant of Jesus**. I for one, knowing the depths of deception of the Church would not find it surprising for church leaders to posit such an assertion.

While this thought may have credibility in the eyes of the inner sanctum leaders of the top 15 men who supervise the dictatorship known as the First Presidency [3] and the Quorum of the Twelve [12]. It would be a leap of faith for them to make such an assertion pending the election and swearing in ceremonies of a president-elect Romney.

Such an assertion would clash with traditional Christianity. It would also clash with Islam and Judaism. It would not be an easy sell to most all of earth's inhabitants but then remember it only took 2% of Russians known as Bolsheviks to capture and control Russia and the Soviet Empire in 1917 and they did not have president-elect control of the massive military might of the United States that would be held by robot-king, Romney!

Nor did they have the advantage of a nation already set up for empire by the maniacal "Manifest Destiny" theories of earlier presidents of the United States.

See: www.americans-united-against-fascist-and-theocratic-government.org also Mormon Conspiracy by Charles Wood; Quest for Empire by Klaus Hansen

16

June 22, 2011

HUNTSMAN OR ROMNEY? CHOOSE YOUR POISON: A SUMMER SOLTICE MESSAGE

Today, after toying with the issue, Jon Huntsman, Jr. former governor of Utah and a fellow Mormon is joining Mitt Romney in a run for the US presidency. I know less about Huntsman than I do about Romney. But what I do know is sufficient to express loud and clear that both or either of them due to Mormon Priesthood oaths are poison to America. Should either of them win the GOP nomination as its candidate and be elected president, it would ensure that America has finally gone the way of the Roman Empire as sure as Caesar's crossing of the Rubicon.

Had either of them had the guts to repudiate Mormonism as I did over 35 years ago when I realized that the ungodly quest for empire of the Mormon church was silently and surreptitiously waiting behind the Western horizon of the Rocky Mountains, then perhaps they could qualify.

Since they haven't repudiated it they must be silent supporters of the plot intended to fulfill founder

Joseph Smith's own quest for empire in 1844 when he ran for president as a fugitive from justice in Missouri.

These men stood by when the church was publicly racist* denying full membership rights of Black male members. These men stood by allowing the church to defeat the Equal Rights Amendment in 1977. These men stand by allowing bright women of the church to be denied equal rights to priesthood possessed by lazy but ego smitten male members of the church claiming a spurious restoration of God's one and only true church [the former "Saints"] which in fact never existed in the first place!

These men gloat over the fact that their wives have taken a blood oath in Mormon Temples to be subservient to them just as sure as women of the Islam culture.

These men smile with a smirk when such brave women as Deborah Laake are reported to have committed suicide after publishing her book "Secret Ceremonies" that openly exposed the temple ceremonies glorifying men and reducing women to a role of slavery. Or their gloating over the excommunication of women's equality crusader Sonia Johnson after they had utilized the Bee lapel pin to organize their subservient wives to defeat the Equal Rights Amendment back in the 1970's thus denying rights which millions of American women need recognized.

These men know and fail to admit that the semi-secret arm of the corporate church engages in damage control and political advancement of the church. That it is capable of contracting for the execution of the blood atonement doctrine and staging such murders as "suicides" like that of Shelton Washington attorney John C. Ragan on Summer Solstice June 21, 1978.

These men cannot lead America while still supporting as truth, the fraudulent Book of Abraham or the proven fraud of the Book of Mormon. They didn't challenge their church leaders earlier to remove racist phrases as, "White and delightsome", from church scriptures or to remove the plural marriage section 132, from the Doctrine and Covenants since it allegedly was repudiated by god vis-à-vis the "manifesto" of Wilford Woodruff and ratified by the church in conference at Salt Lake City, Utah on October 6, 1895.

*Huntsman was only 16 years old when I challenged the church over black racism and I can forgive him for not taking up that issue at that time. However he has had apt opportunity to address the other issues and has failed to do so because of childhood brainwashing.

If these men really want to be president or vice president they need to publically address these issues and repudiate them. Until they can do this they are infected and can only bring poison to democracy like Caesar's crossing of the Rubicon!

17

OBFUSCATING THE MORMON ISSUE:

HEY STUPID! ITS THE PRIESTHOOD LINK NOT THE CHURCH

[This article was written for the 2008 elections but remains germane today 2012]

Mitt Romney's attempt to narrow the religion issue to a, "Shucks folks, there isn't too much difference between a Mormon and a Christian" and the blogging discussions it triggered have obfuscated the real issues. Its like tossing in a packet of aspartame and a little creamer to disguise a bitter cup of coffee.

The Constitution prohibits a litmus test so that a candidate of any persuasion should be able to take a shot at the presidency. That includes Christians, Mormons, Buddhists, Moslems, Jews, Hindus, etc as well as Satanists, *and Atheists!* However, that prohibited litmus test is applied to religious beliefs in general not to a specific political agenda which may be sought by that religion. When politics are hidden within a religion, that agenda becomes fair game for discussion and litmus.

Any attempt to narrow the qualification of a candidate to being a true blue Christian is a political scam not supported by any law and rightly so. Besides, what is a true blue Christian?

From the dawn of history those in political power have consistently merged the two issues of government and religion in an effort to create a manageable constituency. It has been responsible for the dumbing down of the populace and more often for instilling fear as a control device.

The real issue for America is not what religious belief or disbelief a candidate cradles in his/her head but rather does that belief system support or advocate a total separation of itself from the rule of government. What is its political agenda? In a democracy that is a true legitimate concern.

While Mormons do believe that Jesus and Satan were spiritual brothers (as announced by presidential candidate Mike Huckabee) and have a belief of a pre-existence (Before earth mortality) which differs from the other two religions spawned by the Father Abraham story, that doesn't in itself condemn a Mormon as a theoretician.
See: htttp://www.brasschecktv.com/page/233.html

Since the Mormon Church is a relatively new religion, a brief review of its history can easily tell us if it supports true separation of church and state.

I wrote an article published in OpedNews 12/13/07 that discusses the issue as far as Mitt Romney is concerned:
http://www.opednews.com/articles/opedne.doug_wa l_071212_romneys_selective_ig.htm .

In that article I lay out the argument that separation of church and state has not been an attribute of the Mormon Church. Church founder Joseph Smith Jr. Crafted thirteen articles of faith for his church. Among those articles it states: 10. *We believe………* *that Zion (the New Jerusalem) will be built upon the American continent; that Christ will reign personally upon the earth……….* One will have to consider that the building of a New Jerusalem is a political concept when used for the governing of earth's inhabitants. Further identifying the location of that New Jerusalem, Smith declared in 1838 that a location at Far West, Jackson County, Missouri was the site of the original Garden of Eden and it was there that Zion (New Jerusalem) would be built. The order of governing the Mormon Church is one of theocracy. I use that term with full knowledge that the God concept of Mormons does not square with that of Christians, Jews or Muslims. However, it is within the context of the Mormon view of God that the church is claimed to be Theocratic. **The Catholic Church is theocratic but there is no priesthood nexus between the Pope and layman such as JFK as it is between the Mormon "Prophet" and high priesthood candidate Mitt Romney.**

In that context, God The father (of their view) stands at the top of the pyramid. Jesus Christ the son is the

God of this earth. The next officer descending is designated as the current living successor to founder Joseph Smith or the living mouth piece of God in mortality. This individual, currently Thomas S. Monson, is claimed and testified to by all faithful and not so faithful Mormons to be a living breathing prophet who communicates with God on a daily basis. Or as the late "prophet" Spencer Wooley Kimball declared after I challenged the leadership on black priesthood in 1976, "The channels of communication are unchanged". From my perspective that is accurate since there never was a connection.

This first subordinate Priest to Christ has selected two counselors who serve in capacity as the First Presidency. This group of three is surrounded by a Quorum of twelve which constitutes the pool from which upon the death of the current mouthpiece, is selected as the ascending "prophet seer and revelator". Longevity is the selection mode in that God directs it by allowing the senior member to outlive others and thus succeed to the presidency. The doctrine (Law of succession) doesn't explicitly state that God takes the lives of those not healthy enough to outlive one another but it infers that the succession is the will of God!

There are other groups, quorums and councils constituting the "General Authorities". From there in descent are the Presidents of Stakes (Dioceses) and Bishops of Wards (Parishes)
In every instance, the person to fill a vacant office is selected by above "authorities". In fact the Articles of

faith state: 5. "......*all men must be called of God by prophecy and by the laying on of hands by those who are in authority......* "

This is where the order of the priesthood enters into the equation. There are two distinct orders of priesthood: The "Aaronic" or lowest and the "Melchizedek" or higher. There are several degrees in each. The Aaronic has Deacon, Teacher, Priest and Bishop while the Melchizedek has Elder, Seventy and High Priest. The lower concerns temporal matters, the higher spiritual.

An axiom often used is, "The priesthood can exist without the church but the church cannot exist without the priesthood". Paramount to the priesthood is the notion of "KEYS". That is, one individual possess the Keys, the whole ball of wax; the whole nine yards. Smith's claim to priesthood first concerned the Aaronic order when he states that John the Baptist, as a resurrected being, ordained him and associate Oliver Cowdry in Pennsylvania on May 15, 1829 during the time they were involved in "translating" the Book of Mormon. This lower priesthood had no authority to organize the true church.

However To cure this defect, according to Smith, the Melchizedek priesthood was restored to the earth from the days of the New Testament Apostles "sometime**" in June 1829 by the ordination of Smith and Cowdrey under the hands of resurrected Biblical personages Peter, James and John whom Jesus had ordained. The "keys" were laid upon

Smith. It was essential in the Smith narrative that priesthood predated the organization of the church for without its prior re-establishment there would have been no authority to establish the "one and only true church".

Therefore, the President, Prophet, Seer and Revelator of the church holds all powers of priesthood. In order for any man and I mean a male, females excluded, to hold any degree of priesthood he must have it delegated to him through the channels of priesthood which operate independently though in concert with the church. This law of the keys also means that only the prophet can receive revelation for the church. That living person today is Thomas Sterling Monson.

Example: a Bishop is the officer head of a ward (parish) but his calling as a Bishop (being the highest office of the Aaronic priesthood) can only come under ordination to the office of a High Priest (unless he is a direct descendant of biblical Aaron brother of Moses). And so on with his two counselors.

Likewise a Stake (diocese) President and counselors can only hold that office if he/they are an ordained High Priest of the Melchizedek priesthood the keys of which are held by the prophet. So the priesthood is like a tree upon which the leaves of church hang or the skeleton upon which hangs the flesh. On top is the head or the crown. Disassemble the church and the priesthood would still continue to exist.

Mormon detractors to my referenced article attempted to play down the value of a high priest in Mormon layman ministry but that office of priesthood has to be held if one is to function in a higher structured church leadership role. It usually takes years of service and obedience to attain it.

While church members are given the opportunity (and expected) to express consent for any individual who may be appointed ["called"] they have no voice in the selection and are subject to discipline if they should question the selection with a nay vote. Thus works theocracy within Mormonism. The same tactic is employed in dictatorships where the duty to consent is enforced but the right to dissent is nonexistent and punished!

In early Mormon settlements the priesthood order of the church selected the political as well as the military order. In Nauvoo it was Joseph Smith at the helm as President-Prophet, City Mayor and commander Lieutenant General of the 5,000 man militia known as the Nauvoo Legion.

In the Utah territory, before and six years after the Federal territorial Government existed, Brigham Young held the high political office as well as head of the religious order. When Johnston's army was sent to Utah to quell the Mormon Rebellion by President James Buchanan in 1857, the subordinate priesthood/church authorities to Young held the State Militia offices, and they had been organized to fight the U.S. army. "Up Awake Ye Defenders of

Zion" written to the tune of The Red White and Blue was a rallying song of the era.

It was in this context of hyped-up battle anticipation that the Mountain Meadows Massacre happened in 1857 by the territorial militia under the command of Brigham Young. This past September the church finally admitted complicity of the church but blamed it on the local church leaders who were also the militia commanders under the priesthood/church order. In a democracy under chain of command the buck stops with the president but not in a theocracy! *See Mountain Meadows Massacre* (1950) *Juanita Brooks*

We can conclude therefore that when the church had complete control of a geographical area that it functioned as a theocracy. That it was not allowed to do that under the Constitution was a lesson never learned by Smith or Young and only tolerated by successive leaders. In Utah it is still a shadow government.

I have not discussed herein the failed practice known as the United Order which Smith introduced during his theocratic rule. That order required all members of the church to deed all their property to the church (Smith) for redistribution by the church (Smith). That program predated Soviet communism by seventy years but smells of communism. It is still contemplated that in the full bloom of the Kingdom Of God (the Church) that order will be re-instated. The reader can obtain a detailed discussion of the United Order in Ed Decker's latest Book, *MY*

KINGDOM COME ed@saintsalive.com which also discusses at length the Mormon Empire quest! So how does this all square with the presidential candidacy of Mitt Romney?

Romney holds the office of a High priest. He is subordinate to Thomas Sterling Monson who holds the Keys to the priesthood. Romney is dependent upon him for his church/priesthood-active relationship with God. Even as US President, ruling or direction given to him by Monson who speaks for God, as affecting the government of the United States without subjecting himself to discipline for his membership in the Mormon Church. And thus his eternal welfare would be at stake. A dedicated, brainwashed Mormon such as Romney wouldn't even question such a directive. He will consider it the will of God. Now if we didn't have all the evidence of political subterfuge and empire quest that wouldn't be a problem for us.

Should Romney again become a candidate for president, he needs to be asked the question at a first debate, "As a subordinate priesthood holder to the Mormon President, What would you do if you were ordered by the Mormon president to do or not do something that ran counter to the will of the Congress, the courts, the people or of the Constitution?" IT WOULD DO WELL TO PLACE HIM UNDER OATH TO ANSWER THE QUESTION.

Ed Decker, author of *My Kingdom Come* (supra) asks the question: "Suppose that Romney is elected president and the Mormon Church should crown him prophet, seer, revelator and earth king?" *To fit right into the world of the American Empire prepared under Bush! (Italics added are mine.)*

But beyond that question we need to look at exactly what has been "prophesied" by a Mormon leader on the issue of one world government. The Following extracts are quoted verbatim from the pages of MORMON DOCTRINE by Bruce R. Mckonkie, Doctrinarian Son-in-law of past Mormon Prophet, Joseph Fielding Smith. 1966 edition. Under the topic of Kingdom:

Kingdom of God:

"The Church of Jesus Christ of Latter-day Saints (Mormon or LDS) as it is now constituted is the kingdom of God on earth; nothing more needs to be done to establish the kingdom. The Church and kingdom are one and the same." Pg 415

"The Church or kingdom is not a democracy; legislation is not enacted by the body of people comprising the organization; they do not make the laws governing themselves. The Church is a kingdom, The Lord Jesus Christ is the Eternal King and the President of the Church, the mouthpiece of God on earth, is the earthly king. All things come to the Church from the King of the kingdom in heaven through the king of the kingdom on earth". pg 416
"There is of course, the democratic principle of common consent where-under the people may accept or reject what the Lord offers to them.

Acceptance brings salvation; rejection leads to damnation." Pg 416

"During the millennium, the kingdom of God will continue on earth, but in that day it will be both an ecclesiastical and a political kingdom. That is the Church (which is the kingdom) will have the rule and government of the world given to it. When inspired teachers speak of the future setting up of the kingdom of God on earth, they have reference to the millennial day when the "The kingdoms of this world are become the kingdoms of our Lord and his Christ; and he shall reign forever and forever."(Rev. 11:15)

"Daniel also saw the day when *"the saints of the most High (LDS I added)* shall *take and posses the kingdom forever and ever."* (Dan 7:18, 22, 27.) The Prophet (Joseph Smith) prayed that the present ecclesiastical kingdom of God on earth might roll forth that the future political and kingdom of God on earth might come". (Doctrine and Covenants (D&C) 65; Doctrines of Salvation, Vol. 1 pp 229-246.) pg 416

Additional documentation concerns the hearsay prophesy that the day would come when the Constitution would hang by a thread and it would be saved by the "Elders" of but not by the church" www.lightplanet.com/mormons/basic/doctrines/law/c onstitution_eom.htm - 14k -

Considering the fact that the Mormon Church was declared by its founder and, its present day leader that it is an ecclesiastical/ physical/political kingdom, the idea that nothing about it can be discussed in a political sense because it is a religion and therefore out of bounds under litmus prohibition is utter nonsense.

As I stated in the referenced article: Joseph [*http://www.opednews.com/articles/opedne_Doug_ wal71212Romneys* selective_ig.htm] Smith organized the Council of the Fifty of the church to bring about one-world government. The council in turn crowned him "Earth King". Since the church has been identified by the founder as the Kingdom of God on earth, it still exists today and has crowned Thomas Sterling Monson "Earth King" subordinate only to Jesus Christ to act as Vice-Regent of Christ in political and ecclesiastical matters affecting planet Earth!

For a full discussion of this doctrine See: Quest for Empire: The Political Kingdom of God and the Council of Fifty in Mormon History. By KLAUS J. HANSEN. 1967 East Lansing: Michigan State University Press.

Also See: Kingdom on the Mississippi Revisited: Nauvoo ... - by Roger D Launius - 300 pages Equal Rites: The Book of Mormon Masonry ... - by Clyde R Forsberg - 364 pages

In a futile attempt to bring that theocratic condition upon the earth before he died, in the early 1840s Smith dispatched Orson Hyde, a Jewish convert to Mormonism, to the Holy Land to bless and dedicate it for the return of Israel as stated under his tenth of thirteen articles: *"We believe in the literal gathering of Israel and the restoration of the ten* tribes;...."

When that failed to immediately happen, the priesthood repeatedly sent emissaries to bless and re-dedicate the land for the return of the Jews a total of some five times. God didn't seem to be listening. In 1917, 75 years after Orson Hyde's dedication of Palestine for the return of Israel, the Balfour Declaration of November 2, 1917 in the UK addressed to Lord Rothschild spoke in support of the gathering of Israel in Palestine. Finally by fiat, the United Nations in 1948 created the nation of Israel against the interests of the Palestinian people who as descendants of the same Abraham were equally entitled to the land. For that vision of equal rights, we have to discount the dishonesty and subterfuge occasioned by Abraham, Isaac and Jacob in cheating Abraham's Arab descendants of the promise of God. Neither the Mormon Council of the Fifty, the Mormon Prophet nor the United Nations had authority to do such a thing if one is to believe the Old Testament stripped of the dishonesty favoring the descendants of Judah.

With Smith's declaration that the New Jerusalem or Zion would be built at Far West (Jackson County) Missouri, his actions or that of the Council of the YTFIF in dedicating the Holy Land for the return of the Jews would seem to be counterproductive to the scheme of the Missouri plot. However, the scripture, "The law shall go forth from Zion and the word of the Lord from Jerusalem", (Isaiah 2:1-5) (paraphrased) posed a serious hindrance to Smith. Smith identified two separate places to fit into that scripture and the former could not be fulfilled until the latter had been consummated. To him it made sense that Israel would have to be re-established in the Holy Land before the Lord could utter His word (gospel) from Jerusalem and validate laws issuing forth from Zion in America.

In this endeavor, there is a conflict between the Jewish freemasonry Zionists and the Mormon Zionists. The former anticipate that Jerusalem will be the center of world control while Mormons intend it to be in Missouri with themselves in control. [Or in Salt Lake City pending establishment of the temple in "The Garden Of Eden" in Far West (Independence) Missouri.] In Christian end time theories, [eschatology] the world will come to an end with its destruction after it has been subjected to a thousand year rule of peace under Jesus. What has never been discussed in scripture however, exactly….. How is Jesus, the "Prince of Peace" going to maintain peace for a thousand years in the absence of the use of violence or force? Will he hypnotize everyone? Will he hold all life in a state of suspended animation? If so where is their free agency? What good would living like a robot produce?

This is where the idiocy of the failed Third Reich Doctrine (spawned by Hitler's knowledge of Mormonism) and the Mormon "Kingdom of God on Earth" Empire comes into focus. The kingdom will provide the laws (approved by Christ) and the mercenary force to make certain that peace will be maintained at any cost. To hell with individual freedom or collective democracy! Sounds like the Bush doctrine of preemptive strike! [Yes their mercenary force called Danites still exists to this day despite the ignorance of faithful Mormons!]

After the final destruction of the planet, Mormons believe it will be *renewed,* restored *and receive its paradisiacal glory.* [Article 10] That is why it stands unopposed to nuclear war, use of depleted uranium armament, global warming, or the deaths of up to two thirds of earth's inhabitants by disease, plague and famine resulting from capitalist greed. God will renew and fix all this damage to planet earth.

Mormon Church members scream like a stuck pig when they read or hear these truths being expounded. Since they have no idea of the true history of the church, they become inflamed at anyone who dares challenge their brainwashed "learning" and arrogant ego. They have been deeply imbedded with repetitious information assaulted upon the limbic system of their brains without regard for truth. To understand this see:

http://www.humboldt.edu/~tha1/oldbrain.html

Less than one out of 100 and most likely 1,000 devout Mormons (and only three out of ten are devout) know the truth about the history of the faith they are so willing to defend and die for. Yet in their ignorance they always want to place themselves between the critic and the prophet not allowing truth to surface in an honest debate. They have been preemptively armed with scripted denunciations of the detractors which shut down any intelligent discussion. The leaders do not have to answer as they are protected by their deluded followers. Deafening silence has always emanated from the Marble Palace of the Prophet at 47 East South Temple SLC, Utah! It is the Tabernacle of the Wizard of Oz... revisited!

Mitt Romney appears (I use that word cautiously) to be equally ignorant of church history and incapable of sorting fact from fiction thus he will act no different than a marionette dangling on the chains of priesthood "KEYS" held by his superior, Thomas Monson. If he knows then he is deceiving the public.

I would suggest that a one hour public debate be televised between Romney and one of his critics, such as Ed Decker, on the issue of Mormonism/Priesthood; the kingdom of God on earth; the Mormon king and One World government. This should be done before he gets any further in his attempt to obfuscate the issue with contempt for American voters.

18

Dec 11, 2011

Flying Under the Radar: Hiding Romney's Unchristian Credentials

"On the wings of a snow-white dove- he spreads his "Christian" message of love, on the wings of a dove.

If Mitt Romney were a Muslim he would not be participating in the Republican presidential debates. He would know he couldn't do so as Americans would not give him a single nod.

If Mitt Romney were to tell what he needs to tell the American people about his Mormon religion he would know that Americans would not give him any more of a nod than if he were a Muslim.

So he has chosen to fly under the radar. That is an old trick used by politicians and racketeers for millenniums.

THE PLOT

Surreptitiously supporting Mitt in his quest for the most powerful political position on mother earth is the secret co-coordinating agency of the Mormon Church known as the **Council of the Fifty**.

That council was created in June 1844 by Mormon founder Joseph Smith, JR to assist him in his quest for the U.S. presidency as now sought by Romney. At the time of its creation, the council crowned Smith "King' of the earth. The prime mission given the council was/is to mount the Mormon coup d' 'etat. Unfortunately for Smith his quest caused his own death when a gun battle ensued in the Carthage, Illinois jail. It had been a little over a month since Smith was crowned king and had declared his presidential candidacy while still a fugitive from justice in Missouri on a charge of sedition.

Jailed as a fugitive and on charges of destroying a printing press in Nauvoo. Guns had been secretly furnished him and his brother Hiram likely by members of the Council of the Fifty. After Hiram fell mortally wounded and before dying himself, Smith killed two of the gang who were storming up the stair case on the night on June 27th, 1844. He then jumped out the second floor jail window uttering the reputed Masonic distress cry, "O LORD MY GOD!" The gang, whom Smith believed were fellow Masons, instead of answering his plea filled his body with shot as he lay dying. Even though he killed two men, he is called a martyr by Mormons for his religious beliefs. The question remains can a martyr be a martyr when he has just killed two men?

So much for saving their man; the Council of the Fifty made up that deficiency by organizing the two year later Mormon exodus from Nauvoo but giving credit to Brigham Young as the Great colonizer of the Utah Territory.

Once in Utah, the church under the leadership of Young had the freedom for a short time to allow Young, the second crowned "king" of the earth, to run the enterprise as a kingdom. Oddly the Mormons who had traveled west with Young and those who followed for the most part had been brainwashed to accept theocracy as the way of life in the territory. After all that was what god had deemed to be the true method of controlling subjects. Later the people of Utah were only freed from that bondage by actions of the federal government. Today the church leaders and maybe 30 percent of its adherents are still waiting for the day when they can again control and be politically controlled by a Mormon "king".

People who do not know or have no interest in history are doomed to repeat the mistakes of preceding generations.

If Mitt should, be elected president, you can be sure that the semi-secret Mormon Council of the Fifty will become the organizing entity that will assist him in pulling off the coup d'état of making the World the "Kingdom of our God" with the current Mormon Church President already crowned by the Council of the Fifty as the King of the "Kingdom of God on earth". A king to whom Romney has take solemn oaths in a Mormon Temple to be subservient to. In fact he may be crowned king himself by fiat of the top 15 leaders of the church. Otherwise he will be an obedient servant of the Mormon king [Thomas Monson].

THE PLOT TO DISCREDIT McCONKIE'S BOOK MORMON DOCTRINE

Preparatory to deceiving the public, the church in its usual manner has, Like the Grinch, "thought up a lie and thought it up quick", in laying in wait for an expose' such as this article. Be sure they will attempt to establish that Bruce McConkie was a renege writer who overstepped his authority in writing Mormon Doctrine. Although he was a true doctrinarian in every sense of the word, McConkie allowed the top church leaders to critique his book between 1960 and 1965. After spending considerable time with them he revised the book in 1966 so as to conform to the approved content by those leaders. The quotes below are from that revised 1966 book having been vetted by the brethren. So any attempt to defuse the assertions I make will simply backfire in their face.

Although McConkie did a later revision in 1979, it was made to correct the changed policy of Black priesthood. The material quoted here is still in the book although it has been removed from production and sales by the Council of the Fifty in an attempt to deceive the voters and more importantly Mitts fellow contenders for the presidential quest.

Let's look at page 416 [1966 edition] where the "king" thing is written.

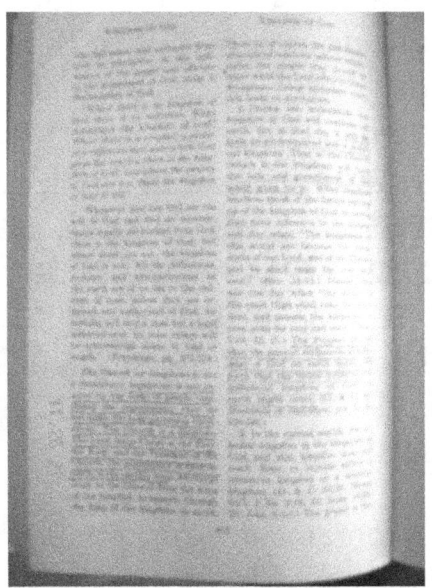

The portion underlined in the left column reads thus:

"The church (or kingdom) is not a democracy, the legislation is not enacted by the body of the people composing the organization; they do not make the laws governing themselves. The Church is a kingdom. The Lord Jesus Christ is the eternal King and <u>the President of the Church, the mouthpiece of God on earth is the earthly king.</u>"

The portion underlined in the right column reads thus:

"During the millennium the kingdom of God will continue on earth. But in that day it will be both an ecclesiastical and political kingdom. That is, <u>the Church (which is the kingdom) will have the rule and government of the world given it........The prophet (*Joseph Smith*) prayed that the present ecclesiastical kingdom might roll forth that the future political and millennial kingdom of God on earth might come"</u> (D&C 65) <u>(Italics added)</u>

Additionally, page 417 contains the same nonsense of Mormon Church supremacy as the Kingdom of God. So there it is. ****see note below.

The clumsy attempt by the church through its secret council to deceive the American public demonstrates the level of honesty we could expect of any Mormon candidate for the office of president. The church needs to come clean, make an apology and publically repudiate the words of the book concerning its plan; that to, "take and posses the kingdom" is a lie and that the goal of Smith and his successors to become president of the United States and "King" of the world is a misdirected delusion. And further, that they will discourage any Mormon member from seeking that public office in order to avoid the shame.

My advice to the moderators who lead the debates: query Mitt Romney and Jon Huntsman on this information and put an end to an attempt to end run the United States Constitution. **This issue is not a litmus test prohibited by the Constitution but rather a long range political goal to eliminate democracy replacing it with theocracy.**

An historical aside:

People should be reminded at least those of us old enough to remember back in 1968 when Mitt's father George ran for president that he withdrew after his statement that he had been "brainwashed" about the Vietnam War. As a presidential candidate that was a death knell for admitting he could be brainwashed.

Unfortunately Mitt, along with a few million others and me included [up until 1976] are or had been brainwashed. Mitt would do well to come to the realization that he is brainwashed as far as Mormonism is concerned and make some apology and amends. He is a nice guy and I would support him if he were free of the Mormon dogma chain around his neck.

View the video:
> http://www.youtube.com/watch?v=nZUA8OSD
> YPg

More information can be obtained at:
> www.americans-united-against-fascist-and-
> theocratic-government.org

19

THE NATIONAL SECURITY AGENCY (NSA) AND THE MORMON CHURCH (LDS): AN UNHOLY ALLIANCE

Aug 31, 2011

S enator Frank Church***, the first chairman of the Senate Intelligence Committee investigating FISA abuses by the NSA made the following dire warning after reviewing the structure and direction of the NSA,

*"That capacity **at any time** could be turned around on **the American people** and **no American would have any privacy left**; such [is] the capability to monitor everything: telephone conversations, telegrams, it doesn't matter. There would be no place to hide. **If government ever became a tyranny, if a Dictator ever took charge in this country** , the technological capacity that the intelligence community has given the government could enable it to impose **total tyranny**, and there would be no way to fight back, because the most careful effort to combine together in resistance to the government, **no matter how privately it was done, is within the reach of the government to know**. Such is the capability of this technology* ". [Emphasis added] NBC Meet the Press August 17, 1976 The Shadow Factory; James Bamford page 344

Since the days when Senator Church spoke those words* communications systems have changed dramatically. Fiber optic cables rest on the sea bed around the world allowing transmissions of voice, email, graphics and music to travel at the speed of light. Additionally the pervasive use of cell phones has changed the way that the intelligence community has risen to meet the challenges.

Today there is very little that is known about peoples of the world that is not residing in massive global databases under the scrutiny of governments. The expansion of technology since 9/11 has grown tremendously and governments are spending billions annually to spy on their own people. The use of contractors in designing computers and programming to build files (dossiers) of citizens is done theoretically at the expense of the victims of the spying [Taxes]. These contractors Have access to all the data gleaned at switching stations in the U.S. and world-wide. AT&T, Verizon and a couple of Israeli firms, Verint and Narus.

Recently I have published an article under the short title, "GOD and MORMONISM: ANOTHER VIEW." In that article I have discussed the 176 year old quest of the Mormon Church to establish its concept of the Kingdom of God on Earth in which the church Priesthood would become the framework for secular governments throughout the world. That is to say the President of the Melchizedek Priesthood, the Mormon Prophet, would become the world dictator. Under him the layers of priesthood would fill in the needed roles of regional and world kingdom officers once their coup had been accomplished.

I briefly discussed the attempt of the Mormon Church to initiate the gathering of files [Dossiers] on its members and on Americans in general as a first step toward the establishment of the Mormon Empire. That effort in the late 60's to early 70's utilized a micro-wave cavity resonation system invented by the Soviets. [Leon Theremin was an inventor and indeed invented a device to make music simply by waving ones hands over it while he lived in the US in the years before WWII. The KGB later kidnapped him back to Russia] The technology was copied and utilized by the church, first at BYU to ferret out gays and against dissidents [this one] and later to defeat the Equal Rights Amendment [ERA]. The visual emblem of the spying was a lapel pin worn by elders of the church [or ladies]   as they mingled with targets.

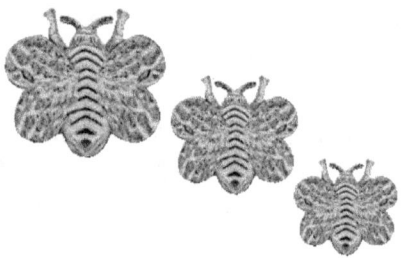

The pins came in three sizes. And had the support of covert technicians monitoring the ongoing intelligence gathering and sending the data to the satellite dish on the top of the Church office building at 50 East North Temple in Salt lake City, Utah where the data would be stored in massive computers on the top 4 floors of the tower. I have discussed this in my book, **"UNDER THE MORMON TREE"**. www.underthemormontree.com

I also discuss in the book a conversation with my father concerning a gap in the system in which communications could not get out of a geographic area between the Coast range in Oregon east to the Cascade mountains and in the south Willamette

Valley in Oregon north to southern Washington. This problem was fixed by erecting a relay station in the Redlands, Oregon area. This area incidentally happened to be where my efforts against the church quest for empire began in 1976. There was also a lot of media speculation about health risks in the area due to micro-wave bombardment.

This undertaking was mind boggling for a small religious organization hell bent on fulfilling the prophecies of its founder Joseph Smith, Jr. It does demonstrate the tenacity with which they go about accomplishing that which they have a deep belief in. It also demonstrates an arrogance of undertaking commensurate with Nazism. The subservient attitude of Mormon Elders to their superiors is reminiscent of the SS boot heel clicking in standing to attention of superiors.

Indeed over the years I have become aware of the similarity between the Mormon quest for empire and the goals of the Third Reich. It is also significant that when Hitler was chastised by the U.S. for his persecution of the Jews that he used a defense that the U.S. had its own history of persecuting Mormons.

At the time, [70's] the system utilized by the church was on the cutting edge of technology and could only be used by entities that were well heeled due to the excessive cost of the system. That was over 30 years ago and technology has moved on dating that system as somewhat obsolete.

I have stated that in January of this year NSA broke ground on a very large facility in Utah in which massive storage of ill gotten world-wide intelligence will be stored. That data will dwarf whatever intelligence the church has acquired since the 1970's. How the Church accomplished this feat, a coup d'état, is a mystery but perhaps not with its false image of patriotism to the U.S. and its agents in the government. Visit www.americans-united-against-fascist-and-theocratic.government.org

Capturing the presidency of the United States by a dedicated Mormon such as Mitt Romney will allow for the consummation of the Mormon Quest for Empire bringing the aggregated intelligence of the local NSA facility under the auspices of the Mormon Church allowing it to fulfill its goal by intimidation, discredit or death of opposition

If that is accomplished, amen to the Constitution of the United States and to the freedom of Americans and peoples of the world. The Second dark ages will have been ushered in.

Americans need to wake up because as Senator Church*** stated in the quotation above, once accomplished there will be no way to resist against government. It will be a kingdom of god by force of arms.

I expressly recommend reading James Bamford's "The Shadow Factory" or view Nova's [PBS], "The Spy Factory" to get the needed depth of understanding of the NSA.

*** Frank Church is also widely quoted in regards to the National Security Agency: "I don't want to see this country ever go across the bridge... I know the capacity that is there to make tyranny total in America, and we must see to it that this agency and all agencies that possess this technology operate within the law and under proper supervision, so that we never cross over that abyss. **That is the abyss from which there is no return**

The 2012 NDAA law signed by Obama is the right of the military to pick up anyone as an alleged terrorist and place them in indefinite detention in a military prison without any right to challenge the detention, is that abyss.

20

Nov 30, 2009

NSA SPYING FILES ON AMERICANS WILL BECOME ACCESSABLE TO MORMON LEADERS AND THAT IS SCARY!

"Quest for Empire: The Political Kingdom of God and the Council of Fifty in *Mormon* History." By Klaus J. Hansen. (East Lansing: Michigan State University 1967) The book is out of print and collector's copies are running about $200.00

In Quest for Empire, Klaus Hansen lays out the diabolical plan of the Mormon leaders since founder Joseph Smith, Jr. had himself crowned King of the Earth by the Council of the Fifty in 1844 not too long before his death.

Every successive leader of the Mormon Church has been also crowned "King" of the Earth. Present Mormon Leader Thomas Monson is also crowned King of the Earth.

The semi-secret Council of the Fifty (spelled backwards in early times, "ytfif "in a clumsy attempt to conceal it) was created by Joseph Smith to prepare the way for the Mormon concept of the Kingdom of God on Earth. It is and has been relentless in that pursuit.

In the late 1950's to early 60's it provided Israel with Uranium ore mined in southern Utah by which Israel, a non signatory to the Nuclear Non-Proliferation Treaty, has developed and presently possesses at least twenty warheads.

It harbors the notion that the day will come when every knee will bow and every tongue confess that Jesus is the Christ and that Jews will cast aside Judaism and become members of the Church of Jesus Christ of latter-day Saints (Mormon). That the great temple of Solomon will be rebuilt on the temple mount in Jerusalem from where the word of the Lord will go forth.

It further harbors the notion that world law will go forth from Zion in Missouri where the "King" of the Mormon notion of an earthly Vice-Regency of Christ, the Mormon Prophet, Seer and Revelator will direct the affairs of a totalitarian global government. Making laws and surreptitiously executing their enforcement using the Blood Atonement * doctrine [justified murder] as needed, those who oppose it will be sinners against God who may need to be killed in order to maintain global subjection to the Mormon Prophet.

This wild ambition has been written about by many authors. Even Mormon doctrinarian Bruce Mconkie in his book **Mormon Doctrine** details all about the longed for establishment of Zion in America with the Mormon prophet at the helm of world government. (See also *Mormon Conspiracy* by Charles Wood)

In 1966 the Mormon Church by way of Mormon Mafia captain Bill Gay [of Howard Hughes infamy] began to create the electronic ability to spy on people world-wide to help bring about the day when the church would be able to eliminate its enemies by which it could more openly pursue its ambition of world domination.

I have written about that subject in my recently published memoirs, **Under the Mormon Tree** *available* from Amazon.com, Kindle and Barnes & Noble

At the time (1966) I was a member of a Mormon ward bishopric and was astounded to learn that a device designed as a bee shaped lapel pin would be given out to certain elders of the church in order to eavesdrop on unsuspecting individuals or groups for the purpose of building up the "Kingdom".

Later the system was used against me and I was able to see firsthand what the device looked like. That is also detailed in **Under the Mormon Tree**. Technically, it is known as a microwave cavity resonator.

The ultimate purpose was to build dossiers on potential enemies against whom the council of the fifty could move to neutralize. All for the purpose establishing the real kingdom of God on earth.

Implementation of the technology had to wait until the church had completed its 47 story international headquarters at 50 east North Temple in Salt Lake City. The top four floors were designed as a fort and storage for the digital records accommodated.

In September 1971 I took my oldest daughter to start her studies at BYU in Provo Utah. Due to an automotive breakdown on my way back toward Salt Lake City, I was able to have the time to visit with my old Boss, Julian Cannon, at the church building department.

He was also in charge of the belated tower construction and was being forced into retirement upon completion of all but the top four floors. When asked what those floors were for he replied that he had no improvement plans. When I asked why not he responded, "Beats the hell out of me but they are building it like a fort!"

The use of the info gained from the technology was first used to ferret out gay students at BYU. Six of whom committed suicide after a meeting with Spencer W. Kimball. By 1975 the technology was in full operation as discussed in **Under the Mormon Tree.**

How much digital info on Americans and others is presently stored in the equipment on those top floors of world headquarters can only be guessed at. It is without a doubt obtained sans court order and all in violation of the constitutional privacy rights of Americans. Info collected from other locations of the world likewise is illegal.

If the reader thinks that is scary information; consider what is presently being developed to augment those digital records in the state of Utah!

The National Security Agency (NSA) is building a 1.5 million square feet cyber storage facility in Utah costing 1.6 Billion Dollars. See:

http://www.informationweek.com/news/government /security/showArticle.jhtml?articleID=221100260

The stated purpose is the same as the Mormon spying; to know who to move against when the occasion arises: Those who would oppose fascist control of the world.

Anyone who knows anything about the tight Mormon control over federal agencies in Utah will understand that by building the facility there the Mormon Church and its Council of the Fifty will have unfettered access to the information stored in that building.

The efforts of Mormon Senators Robert Bennett and Orin Hatch have paid off handsomely for this storage facility to be located in Utah. It matters not to them that the digital information is gleaned from NSA unauthorized interception of the private communications of Americans. To them it is no different than what the secret agency of the church has been doing for the past forty years from the state of Utah with its microwave spying technology.

For those who wish to see the Mormon Church succeed in its quest for Empire, do nothing but clap your hands!

For those of us who know the dishonest nature of Mormon racketeering we should be in the streets objecting to this travesty on the citizens of the United States! The Dark Ages of the Catholic hierarchical control of the world will be seen to be as child's play as against the sanctimonious arrogant attitude of Mormon Elders and their heel clicking obedience to the Great Imposter: God's Mormon Vice-Regent on planet EARTH!

* Blood atonement saves sinners because the blood of Christ doesn't cover them. Under the doctrine having their bloodshed by others covers their forgiveness.

21

THE SINISTER ENTITY BEHIND THE CHRISTIAN FACADE OF MORMONISM

Jan 29, 2010

Ask any good Mormon and he/she will tell you that the Church of Jesus Christ of Latter-Day Saints is run by A Christian Prophet, Seer, Revelator head of the church and his two counselors backed up by a group of Christian men known as the "Apostles'. Nothing could be further from the truth.

On April 6th 1976 I and my associates encountered unmistakable evidence of a mafia-like presence on Temple Square in Salt Lake City, Utah. We determined that a corrupt racketeering organization was the real power of the church and that the church leaders were pawns, puppets or willing participants of that criminal entity.

Using religion as a front has been the modus operandi of crooks and scoundrels from the earliest times of earth's history. The reason being the eager credulity of humans to fall prey to any claims that "emanate" from "God".

Intellectuals of the church; many of whom over the years have written articles and letters to the leaders of the church attempting to reason with them have been dismayed by the total silence coming from those leaders. In fact the offices of the First Presidency and the Quorum of the Twelve are similar to the black hole theories of astrophysics when it comes to answering their critics.

Their offices have been alluded to as the "Marble Palace Mob" and the "Temple of Deafening Silence". Mormons who have been faithful members doing their mind/time occupying allegiance to the church are of course the most desirous kind of membership blindly following the leaders, never questioning anything.

However, for a small percentage of members who have broadened their studies to the point that they wish to request a fuller examination of the issues of the faith which are not covered in the stilted and programmed plan of salvation, continued membership becomes a problem for them.

Descendants of early pioneers to the Salt Lake valley who have been so culturally bonded to the church because it is not merely a religion but a way of life; find that socially, it is better to remain silent and not mince words with other members for fear that they may become dis-fellowshipped or excommunicated resulting in social ostracism from the church and hence the society in which they have lived their entire lives. For them the cost of expressing intellectual integrity is too high a price to pay. Within the church there exists a significant group of such persons who privately will thank the visible dissident for his or her contribution to the cause for enlightenment while they, themselves, dare not be visible and for good cause.

Few others who were descendants of early converts have taken the risk of suffering excommunication for their visible outspoken efforts to bring intelligence, questioning debate and new learning into the church to correct perceived errors. These individuals both men and women suffered the rebuke of the local elders of the church by way of excommunication but never heard one word directly from the top leaders of the church to whom they had addressed their concerns.

Among those we can name C.D. McBride of Logan, Utah who was a boyhood playmate of the past church president Spencer Kimball: G.T. Harrison of Orem, Utah who challenged the leaders on the changing history and doctrines of the church only to be excommunicated and Dr. John Fitzgerald of Holladay, Utah who wrote letters to the editor of the Salt Lake Tribune challenging the church on its then racism only to be excommunicated. Each of these men had performed a mission for the church in their youth but like so many other returned missionaries, later learn the falsehood of the Mormon claim which they had preached and promoted.

In every case an effort is later made to discredit these men with assertions of moral infidelity as the reason for excommunication rather than admit to doctrinal disputes with the church leaders.

The church is not interested in correcting anything that is working for them and the leaders can ill afford to openly engage in any debate with dissidents. For to do so would expose the lack of deep understanding of the doctrines they espouse. Indeed, they have no need to come out in public debate, for they have juniors, duped by elders in the thousands if not millions, who are more than willing to lay down their life in the defense of the non-answering leaders. They are in fact surrounded by those defenders and as a result can retreat to their temple of deafening silence with apparent impunity.

But it is also apparent that discipline of anyone who publicly challenges the Mormon position or may appear to have gotten the upper hand will be dealt with in a way that a lesson will be taught that those persons will never forget and will likely cause them to retreat to their own temple of silence for fear of having even greater punishment inflicted upon them including untimely death itself.

While the public may observe the disrepute being inflicted upon those individuals it will never know who was the moving power behind such an event for in each case the punishment will never be identified as coming from an entity of the church or the reasons given for it. It is possible the candidate for public discredit may never know himself exactly why he was being punished.

In 1982, author John Gardner published a fiction book, MICKELSSON'S GHOSTS. The story was about a college professor who bought an old house in Pennsylvania and went through the process of remodeling it only to find hidden within its walls evidence of the life of Joseph Smith, Jr. the founder of Mormonism. The professor learned of the existence of killer Danites of the church and in fact discovered that some of his own college faculty were indeed Danites.

In time, as the professor probed into the issue, he was deliberately run off the road on his bicycle and killed. While of course the book was fiction, Gardner did rail against the historically correct existence of Danites within the church and enlarged the theme to a point of belief. Shortly after the book was published, Gardner, a motorcycle enthusiast was run off the road and killed in the same manner as the hero of his book.

The well known massacre of the 1857 Fancher wagon train at Mountain Meadows in southern Utah is but one example of the work of criminal killers within the Mormon Church. Recently the church admitted its complicity yet blamed in on the elders in southern Utah. Yet anyone who knows anything about the political structure knows full well that an atrocity of that nature could never have happened without the sanction of Brigham Young. Not often known was the escape on foot after darkness of two men from the Fancher Train. After the massacre at Mountain Meadows, elders of the church rode their horses to locate these escaping men and upon finding them, slit their throats.

It took the church over a hundred twenty years to allow the Utah Government to establish a formal historical site of the Massacre. And then only upon the insistence of the descendants of the few children who were spared the fate of their older brothers and sisters and parents of being shot at point blank range after surrendering their weapons in a devious offer of protection by Mormon John Doyle Lee, a Danite and local church leader.

The Springville murders were another example of criminally sanctioned atrocities by the church against dissidents attempting to leave the Utah territory.

The so-called Morrisite war in Ogden Canyon, Utah, where dissident Mormons were laid siege against by men under authority of Brigham Young. Cannons were used to blow apart their fortification.

The Gunnison survey party was massacred near Delta Utah as they surveyed the route for the transcontinental railroad. An historical marker was made and is likely (as it was when I took a picture in 1993) in a state of vandalized desecration.

The church pretty much dominates the Salt Lake Police Department and any number of actions in defense of the "pristine" image of the church is carried on by undercover operatives of the PD. U.S. Representative Allen Howe was set up for an arrest and conviction for soliciting by female officers of the police because he voted against the will of the church. Humiliation was so great for Howe afterwards, that he was buried in a secret grave for fear that it would be desecrated by the criminally insane order of the church.

The kidnapping of Howard Hughes by the so-called Mormon Mafia led by recently deceased Bill Gay is another story of intrigue which I outlined in the March-April 1978 issue of the Millennial Messenger* leading to capitulation on the part of the church to the cause of black priesthood ordination.

John Meier was an aide to Howard Hughes and he had been set up by Bill Gay under the guise of Summa Corporation as a defendant in a lawsuit filed in Salt Lake City. An attempt was made to extradite John from Vancouver, Canada. In an effort to obtain John's presence in Utah, the sinister entity of Mormonism attacked and discredited John's Vancouver BC attorney in a shameful way as reported to me by the Member of Parliament [MP] for Delta, BC. Read more in **_Under the Mormon Tree_**

Two men were involved with me at the time of the ordination of a black man to priesthood in a pool at a motel in downtown Portland, Oregon April 2nd, 1976. One man - Darrell Lee - was an associate attorney and was a non participant but we had shared the same office letterhead. The other, John Evans, was an aviator and flight instructor and he did participate with me at a Conference in Salt Lake City on April 6, 1976. When Evans refused to identify himself outside

Temple Square to the media, the church named him as Darrell Lee.

Being an attorney, Darrell saw an opportunity to sue for slander and did so naming the church, Salt Lake PD, News wire services and local Portland area newspapers as defendants. The source for the false naming of Lee was the church as they took the name from the joint letterhead (which I had used in a communication with the church presidency) and making a giant leap in speculation gave it out to the media. Ultimately the case, being a res ipsa [it speaks for itself] situation, an out of court settlement was agreed upon and the record sealed.

Following that settlement, Lee with an associate invested in the Portland Meadows Race track in Portland, Oregon. Subsequently, an evil rumor was widely circulated that Lee had pilfered Jockey Trust fund monies.

There was no proof offering of the allegations but the issue was a matter of great publicity in the Portland area. Lee and his wife Vicky were barred from stepping foot on the race track again even though they were innocent of any charges.

Lee and his wife have pretty much gone into seclusion, having been taught a lesson by the anonymous criminal entity of the Mormon Church and likely have not connected the dots. I have regretted having used an office letterhead in my prior correspondence with church leaders whereby his name could have arisen in the first place.

Concurrently with Lee's problems, an ugly public rumor was laid against John Evans as the operator of Vancouver Aviation. Again no proof of wrongdoing was presented but the discredit drove John to give up his interest in the aviation enterprise and he moved to Hillsboro, Oregon where he did some flight instructing and engaged in the buying and selling of aircraft; later driving a school bus to augment income. John died at age 72 on New Year's Day 2003 having been another victim of the Mormon criminal enterprise.

Mormons or other residents of the Portland-Vancouver area, while aware of the scandals, had not a clue that the criminal entity of the Mormon Church was behind it and getting even with both of these men.

Earlier in Shelton, Washington on June 21, 1978, an assassin of the Danite order had shot an attorney in the back of the head as an apparent suicide in an elaborate scheme to set me up for discredit. That issue is presently before the criminal division of the IRS upon a request to deprive the church of its tax exemption status due to its racketeering.

Several other attempts had been made to discredit me, but I always seemed to be ahead of them. Indeed, if the evil church entity wants to silence me it will hereafter expose itself in the process.

The list of victims of the criminal conspiracy of Mormonism is endless and I could add more than I have. Being a fanatical keeper of records, all records of the activity of the sinister side of Mormonism are available to investigators upon subpoena. Because of a literal belief that these records are the books out of which they, the church leaders, will be judged by God, the church is in an extremely vulnerable position. I happen to be privy to knowledge of access of those records which I will share with Federal investigators when the time is ripe.

Any reader can get the full story by acquiring my memoirs, **Under the Mormon Tree** available from Amazon.com, Kindle and Barnes and Noble

What stands out clear is that Mormon leaders are Satanic not Christian and their goal by subterfuge is to gain control over the earth as a corrupt ecclesiastical entity directing world government by theocracy. It has been referred to as the Mormon Corporate Empire, which is Fascism at its worst! All references to Trilateralists, Bilderbergs, Rothchilds, etc. are minor as compared to the threat of a Mormon conquest.

Most sad is the total ignorance of the sinister side by faithful members of the church who never in their lifetime have challenged church leaders in any aspect of the church. Because of that they have never known and have never experienced the sinister side of Mormonism. Thus what I have described in this article is outrageous to them. If they knew the truth they would dump the church in a New York minute!

22

9-11 and the Mormon-Mossad-CIA Connection

April 02, 2009

A recent Pentagon paper accidentally exposed the fact that Israel has a nuclear bomb. Truth is that they have an estimated sixty warheads. Israel is non signatory to the Nuclear Non-Proliferation Treaty [NNPT] and behind that blanket of secrecy they have created a capacity to destroy their Arab cousins if push comes to shove. The fallout from such action would of course be self defeating both politically and radiation wise.

On the other hand Iran is signatory to NNPT and while they have openly discussed development of nuclear energy so as to not exhaust their oil reserves, they have been criticized with claims from the West that the real ambition is to develop a nuclear war head. At this point in time neither state has a known rocket delivery system capable of reaching the other. It would be foolish of the United States or Russia to furnish a delivery system to either.

Under terms of the NNPT, peaceful use of nuclear energy is OK. Iran has signed on but Israel has not. One has to ask why Israel offers no transparency while Iran is open to inspection.

With such now non-secrecy of possession of a nuke capacity by Israel, one could not blame Iran if it were in fact pursuing an offset to nuclear blackmail from Israel, i.e., mutually assured destruction [MAD].

The United States was at the fore-front of efforts to create the state of Israel and to defend it against its Arab neighbors. It took only 11 minutes for the US to ratify the UN resolution creating Israel in 1948. All this has to do with the Christian concept of a redeemable Israel for the death of Christ with an expectation of a nuclear holocaust in the Middle East ending in a rapture and second coming of Jesus, king of the Jews who are expected to finally accept him as their long awaited Shiloh/Redeemer/King.

Mormons are aligned in that concept with one slight deviation. They believe that Zion will be built upon the North American continent at a place specific in Missouri and that Mormon leaders will become vice Regents of Christ ruling earth [The law shall go forth from Zion (in America) and the word of the Lord from Jerusalem] !

The church in fact has taken steps to implement that concept beginning as early as 1843 when it sent an emissary, Orson Hyde, to Palestine to dedicate the land for the return of Jews. Expecting it to happen soon thereafter, they were disappointed when it didn't, later sending emissaries several times to re-dedicate the land.

The biblical prophesies of such an event being fulfilled is central to Mormon doctrine and essential as a catalyst to propel it toward a delusional destiny of becoming the civil/theocratic world government.

The success of Jews returning to the Holy Land creating prophetic conflict with their Abrahamic cousins who were deceitfully deprived of the full inheritance of the estate of Abraham and promises of the Biblical God is an adventure of significant importance to Mormons but more importantly to their dictatorial leaders. It all has to do with unbridled ego and sense of importance. It is no wonder then that the secret order existing within the higher echelons of the church [Danites/ Council of the Fifty] have worked hand in glove with Mossad.

The posture and thinking of Mormons toward Israel is well depicted by the narrative within W. Cleon Skousen's book, **Fantastic Victory**, published shortly after the 1967 six day war.

The establishment of a branch of Brigham Young University in Israel created a legitimate front for covert activities of the secret/CIA element of the church. It is from there that Mormon world political interests are promoted and pursued lobbying the Israeli government to pursue its unenlightened, inhuman activities under Mosaic Law of an eye for an eye philosophy against Arab states and the deprived Palestinian people.

The doctrine of pre-emptive strike as recently used by the US in Iraq is a reversal of that law in that in anticipation of the enemy striking, the retaliation is delivered first. We have seen justification for such criminal behavior uttered by the last Administration in regards to the attacks by Israel in preemptively destroying nuclear plants under construction in Iraq in the early 90's and in Syria as late as 2007.

The first public awareness of the nexus between Mossad and Mormon secret agents was published by Norman Mailer in **A Harlot High and Low** in the 70's when a reconditioned WWII Liberty ship was hijacked on the Thames River in London by Mossad agents. The ship had a cargo of uranium ore that had been originally mined in southern Utah. The details of that intrigue were published in an earlier article on OpedNews it involved the Utah Corporation which mines the surface of Australia as well as Chile.

I mentioned that Secret elements of the church conspired with the CIA to overthrow democratically elected president Allende of Chile so that the business interests of the church could continue uninterrupted by the then recent action of Allende in nationalizing the mines in Chile.

 The most recent exposure of that nexus came within the framework of the 9-11 event. Being pre-informed if not directly involved in the plans for destroying the Twin Towers as well as Building 7 on September 11,

2001 is reported by advice given to Mormons working in the World Trade Center to not show up for work that day.

An NGO [non-government organization] called **The Project For the New American Century** published a white paper called "Rebuilding America's Defenses" in September 2000 just before the questionable November elections putting Bush JR into office. The paper called for a war with Iraq in the concept of a "New Pearl Harbor"

All evidence indicates that 9-11 was a planned operation of Mossad utilizing all the intelligence it had in causing the pre-planting of explosives within all 3 buildings well in advance of that fateful day. Mossad agents were arrested after the event upon suspicions of citizens who watched them waiting with digital cameras on tripods aimed at the twin towers long before any aircraft struck them. The displayed actions of these Mossad agents was video taped by patriot observers especially when they jumped and shouted with joy at seeing the collapse of the towers and resulting deaths of 3,000 people.

These same Mossad agents were released under order of the Federal government and allowed to fly back to Israel thus implicating not only Mossad and Mormon agents but the Bush Administration as well. 9-11 was a well planned and choreographed false flag operation but not only by some turbaned Arabs in a cave in Afghanistan!

The nexus between the church and the Bush Administration has been documented by the pressure placed on the church from a personal visit by Bush to church headquarters in Salt Lake City prior to the forced retirement of BYU physics professor Steven Jones in late 2006. Jones was/is in the forefront of scientifically establishing a conspiracy to destroy the World trade Center by pre planted explosives. He is just doing what church founder Smith predicted elders of the church would do in saving the Constitution.

Further nexus of the Bush administration lay in the fact that a very large victim's compensation fund was available immediately after 9-11 [waiting in the wings for 9-11 to happen along with the Patriot Act] by which silence of those victims would be purchased by the government to quell legal claims for wrongful death. Victim's failure to release all claims for wrongful death resulted in denial of payment from the fund.

If, in fact, the 9-11 attack was simply and solely an act of war by a foreign entity no victim's claims could be brought against the US government. So why insist on a stand down by victims unless there was complicity by the government [CIA] and other individuals and entities such as Israel's Mossad and the Mormon Church among them?

A few smart victims refused to be bought off and they stand to profit greatly when criminal conspiracy charges for murder are brought against the co-conspirators of 9-11.

Conviction will establish 9-11 to be an act of mass murder not an act of war. It will also open the window of the statute of limitations for actions for wrongful death. While the US government is basically bankrupt, Members of the Bush Administration are not nor is Israel or the Mormon Church.

It is encouraging to see that Spain will likely prosecute members of the Bush Administration for torture as is noted in news headlines today. Hopefully all the links to the bogus war on terror will be exposed.

All you good but ignorant Mormon members who want to stand up and defend your leaders against these charges need to be silent for you will be entering an arena in which you have absolutely no knowledge. Indeed if you do, you will likely be guilty of being an accessory after the fact. A word to the wise is to keep your own counsel and let church leaders make their own defense after all they are big boys!

However, if you are in any way complicit in this tragic criminal conspiracy please do speak up it may get you some immunity.

MORMON HOPE

"O say what is truth?
Tis the fairest gem,
To which mortals and
Gods may aspire!"
But Mormon Church Leaders,
In all that they do,
Merely lie, cover-up and conspire.
For truth deals them out
With a sure deadly blow
So-retreat to the sanctuary of silence!
No answers may not come to the
Truth seeking soul,
For they're lost in a deep muddy mire!
Awake O you "saints" from your
Mind--- numbing sleep.......
Take a good look at your hope!
You'll find that its made out of
Fraud and deceit
Tied-up with some old rotten rope!

Millennial Messenger March-April 1978)

23

MONSTEROUS MALIGNANCY OF 1999 MORMON CHURCH HANDBOOK OF INSTRUCTONS

March 21, 2010

Recently, while surfing the internet, I discovered I could open Book 1 of a two Book set of instructions to the male priesthood hierarchy of the Mormon Church. Reading it I discovered what I consider the most insipid collection of control mechanisms designed to render a Mormon member, man or woman to the absolute role of a duped obedient robot under the leaders of the church particularly the so-called First Presidency currently headed by Thomas Sterling Monson. The official title for Book one is CHURCH HANDBOOK OF INSTRUCTIONS.

While the document(s) have been noted "All rights reserved" the presumption is that it is copyrighted even though a symbol does not appear. Ten years ago a short legal skirmish over copyright infringement was held between the Church through its Intellectual Reserve Corporation that holds all copyrights for the church and Sandra and Jerold Tanner and their Utah Lighthouse Ministry in 1999 and 2000, As I recall the issue was over an earlier publication which may not have been properly copyrighted.

The church asked for a temporary restraining order and the U.S. District court judge coined a phrase "Contributory Infringement" later stricken from the Court Record by settlement. Such a term suggested that anyone who may pass on the link to another who might actually use the copyrighted material in a manner violating the copyright would be liable for "contributing" to infringement. Since the issue was settled and no appeal was taken to the appeals court ratifying the use of the coined phrase it no longer is a viable legal phrase.

As with any copyrighted material, merely reading it does not violate the copyright. Obviously reading the book is not a right reserved to the publisher i.e.; the church.

As a result of the lawsuit many angered members and ex-members of the church responded by posting the books on the internet for downloading. I found a site in Amsterdam!

There are numerous sites around the world where the book can be opened and viewed. I would not advise downloading. However it is not likely that one can use Microsoft Internet Explorer as terminal blocks have been posted to prevent access to many of the sites. I discovered even Goggle will turn a surfer in circles to prevent access to the download sites. Open source browsers such as Firebox will at the present get a surfer access.

The church claims that the publication of the handbook is neither for public consumption nor for open access to its twelve million plus members but rather only for use by the hierarchal order of the church priesthood because it contains "sensitive" instruction intended only for persons in leadership positions to direct the affairs of the church.

It is distributed in a need to know descending order of priesthood. Since Book 2 deals with auxiliary organizations which may include women or girls only those parts of the instructions are intended for use by them. And the priesthood is directed to just Xerox those portions from the books to give to female leaders and also to limited male leaders of male organizations, such as Aaronic priesthood Quorums, Boy Scouts and Young men's and Young women's Associations. Upon retiring from any church position ,it is expected that the materials be given to a successor or to an immediate superior leader in order to keep the information out of unsuspecting hands of members.

What I see as a former member of a Bishopric and an attorney is a published plan of ignorant conspiracy to dupe members and potential members [Investigators] into a life of subservient slavery to the church leadership. While the language is couched in "kindness" the purpose is clear to rip away the individual freedoms of a member or potential member otherwise protected by civil law by following in a pattern of mind control to ideas and principles purported as "Christian" but which can only be described as dark sided in concept. The need for repentance of any member violating any moral code of the church with it holding the false carrot of eternal glory in the afterlife is the method for mentally beating into shape the wayward initiate to the mind control plan. It is not to make the member a better Christian but to secure the leaders in perpetual mind control.

For well over forty years I have kept a general handbook of instructions dated from 1968 when I served in a local Bishopric. In it I find no such in-depth detailed conspiracy to control the minds of members. Nor was the book copyrighted to prevent anyone from having it or assessing it. While I knew the church was corrupt when I challenged it on the racism of Black priesthood denial in 1976, I never dreamed it would go this far to publish its conspiratorial plan for slavery under the guise of "religion".

This is where the gutsy stuff of the church dealing with Transvestites, Gays and Lesbians is published. The leaders speak as if they were the ultimate authority upon the earth for matters which actually escape their collective intelligence. So we have ignorant/prejudiced men pretending to speak for God without any real authority except for superstitious beginnings in a river in Pennsylvania followed by a claim of more ordination but without record!

I recommend that word be passed around to surf and find these books of contemptible conspiracy to control the lives not only of its comparative few members but also of the lives of earths estimated 360 million people who by birth, not choice, find themselves in the general category of "GAYS" and who outnumber worldwide Mormons by a 28:1 majority. It is also a plan for the control of all of earth's inhabitants [7.3 Billion] when the church succeeds in overthrowing governments [by deception] to implement its "Kingdom of God on Earth". Now you know why it has missionaries all around the world! So from reading it anyone can get a glimpse of citizen life [or death] in a future world dominated by the church. It truly would be a return to the dark ages of mankind. God help us!

No person today should consider joining the church before they have read the Handbook of Instructions to know the mind control they will be under. Full disclosure to investigators would be entirely appropriate for them to make an informed judgment for future life. All members of the church should read it but it really would make little difference to the duped faithful so I see no problem there.

Indeed it would behoove the church to save its secrets for the temples* and open handbooks one and two to retail sales and thus satisfy the secrecy hunger of anyone.

Time to wake up world! The monster of Mormonism has shown its head. Find a site and view the conspiracy!

Browse: **LDS HANDBOOK OF INSTRUCTIONS-1**. No, I won't post the website! You will have to first find it on your own. Contact me for clues if you experience real difficulty.

Another way to educate one's self is to obtain my book, UNDER THE MORMON TREE from Amazon.com.

* [*but even there only duped members keep the secret as there are a number of sites on the internet that show what are "sacred" secrets*]

24

BRINGING SENSE TO TAX EXEMPTION: A COMING MORMON DILEMMA

October 23, 2009

As a twenty-two year old kid missionary in 1951, I was acting architect for the British Mission of the Mormon Church. The last project that was handed to me was planning a design for a Temple of the church to be built in London.

The mission president at the time, Stayner Richards, had correctly realized that after over a century of Mormon missionary work in the UK that there was insufficient membership build-up to allow for organization of Stakes And Wards of the church which is the mature development of the church concept of Zion. The reason being that the ceremonies of temple blessings could not be obtained in the UK and so new members would immigrate to Utah where they could obtain these blessings.

One day in the summer of 1951 while accompanying Richards on a train trip from London to Liverpool (future home of the Beetles) he stated these concerns to me and requested I commence preparing schematic drawings for a temple to be built in London. I have documented that effort in my biography, *Under the Mormon Tree.* Returning to the States by air in December 1951, I was urgently directed to present my materials to Mormon President David O. McKay at church headquarters in Salt Lake City at which point I would have an honorable discharge of my mission.

This was accomplished and the very first approval for a temple outside the Western Hemisphere (except Hawaii) was a landmark in church growth. The site I had selected was not used but a site some miles south of London was later selected and in 1958 a temple was built there.

Twenty odd years after my efforts to design and select the temple site in London I was in a personal position to have completely devalued the temple and its ceremonies so that I was glad that the London Temple as built and located did not have my hand prints on it.

Between 1994 and 1998, a second temple known as the Preston Temple was built and dedicated in Northwestern England. It was built as was the London temple within a complex of buildings such as a chapel complex and housing for temple workers and its Patrons.

Temple Patrons are members of the church who have passed strict investigation as to morals, strength of church membership and the most important, being a full tithe payer to the church treasury. The tithe represents a full ten percent of gross income before any governmental taxes are deducted. A member in otherwise good standing but failing the full tithe requirement is denied a pass from the local church hierarchy to receive a Temple recommend. Sometimes a member of the hierarchy will befriend a member and pass on the full tithe requirement anyway.

Probably less than 30% of Mormons are full tithe payers and therefore 70% are ineligible for the temple recommend. Boiled down to the lowest denominator, only members who have paid the price for the "Blessings" of the temple are allowed in it. These blessings include the right to be married by the Holy Priesthood of God for time and all eternity and to have their children and ancestors "sealed" to them in an endless family chain for all eternity.

Prior to those ceremonies, each patron receives the right of endowment to wear holy underwear of regulation design sold by the church which is said to ward off the evil one. Afterward, each patron may return to the temple and do proxy work for each of their ancestry provided they continue to obtain the Temple Recommend each year by paying a full tithing. It is very similar to the privilege to operate a car upon the highways by purchasing an annual registration. The proxy work consists of going through the temple ceremonies in the name of a dead ancestor. Women patrons for women and men as patrons for men. As such, all dead ancestors can, if they elect, become Mormons in the afterlife and have eternal marriage, give birth to and raise spirit babies and ultimately become Gods.

In the UK a problem arose in relation to the real property taxes which are levied upon all land of the crown deeded in fee simple as a mini proportionate rent for the land. Only the Sovereign actually owns land and leases it to the deed holder of title of possession. Pay the annual tax and one keeps possession. Refusal to pay the tax forfeits it to the Sovereign!

Generally, properties that are used for religious worship are exempted from property taxes which of course increases a burden of governmental support on taxpayers.

In 2008 after a protracted period of litigation, tax exemption was denied the Mormon Church for the Preston Temple and certain ancillary structures. The final appeal can be read here:

http://www.publications.parliament.uk/pa/ld200708/ldjudgmt/jd080730/gallag-1.htm

In analyzing the pertinent law, it was determined that only structures which were open to public religious services were exempt from the tax. It was ruled that since the public in general and Mormons who failed to pay tithe were denied access to the temple that it failed to meet the test of being open to public worship.

Thus two large Temples expensively endowed are denied a tax exemption in the UK. What amount of tax is paid is not known however it would be substantial. From my vantage point I would argue that all Mormon Temples in whatever country built should likewise be taxed for the benefit of local government. Properly analyzed all Mormon Temples are an imposition upon the public and can in no way be determined to provide a substitute public service to local governments saving that government the costs of providing health or public welfare which is the rational by which tax exemption is granted.

The only benefit gained of Mormon Temples is gained by the church (money). The temple ceremonies in no way substitute for any public good that might otherwise be provided by government. Indeed it would be out of character if not illegal for government to claim that it has any authority to grant the promise of the Celestial Kingdom to any person in or out of a religious setting.

Closely examined, the promised rewards of the temple ostensibly gained by patrons are akin to buying a share in the Brooklyn Bridge. It is all tin foil, mirrors and gross B.S. ....promises that can never be kept and will never be kept. So if the patrons feel they have actually gained anything from committing to temple requirements, let the church at least pay back to local governments a portion of its gain from the temple scheme.

I would advocate that very soon local governments wise up to the scam that has been dumped on them and claim their fair share of the enterprise by assessing real and personal property taxes on all Mormon temples not only in the United States but throughout the world.

In a future article I will deal with AFTOR, Americans For Taxing Organized Religion, its past and future efforts to remove Federal tax exemption from individual income donated to organized religion.

A test flight of AFTOR was launched 13 years ago and it is time to bring it on again.

25

THE MORMON GOD: A SUPER STAR STUD

January 25, 2009 at 14:23:01

MITT ROMNEY NEEDS TO DO SOME MATH!
AMERICANS NEED TO CONSIDER THIS DOCTRINE
WHEN EVALUATING MORMON CREDIBILITY IN ITS
INTERFERNCE WITH HOMOSEXUAL RIGHTS AND   ITS
QUEST FOR EMPIRE

"In the heavens are parents single?
No, the thought makes reason stare!
Truth is reason, truth eternal
Tells me I've a mother there!"
Mormon Hymn

ETERNAL MARRIAGE OR PHALLIC FANTASY?

Mormon doctrine teaches that all of earth's inhabitants were born in the spirit world before becoming candidates for earth mortality and that God and His plural wives produced those spirit children in the same manner as it happens in mortality. That is to say by way of sexual intercourse. The doctrine also teaches that "worthy" males and females will inherit the "Celestial Kingdom" (where God dwells) and become gods and goddesses to create worlds and fill them with people in the same manner as God and his predecessors have.

This doctrine (story) is taught to every faithful member from childhood on and becomes one of the guiding stars of Mormon theology. As a result, even though polygamy has been officially removed from the observed practices of the church since the 1890 Manifesto* of church president Wilford Woodruff, most every Mormon male is looking forward to the day when the practice can be re-instated. **[* Church property had been escheated (seized) by the US government as a penalty for violating territorial law banning polygamy. This manifesto got it back!]**

In the meantime, the custom of marriage in a temple is promoted and practiced so that those faithful young Mormon couples will have a head start toward that doctrinal goal when they have passed the veil of tears. The number of times annually when temple marriages are solemnized is in the thousands.

In order to check out the rationality of that eternal marriage/procreation doctrine, I recently did some surfing/calculating on the issue of how many humans had been on earth since the First Stone Age. I guessed the results might show an irrationality of the phallic fantasy of Mormon men.

The study could not be accurate without including an additional 1/3rd of the calculated actual world population to cover the group that was cast out of heaven as followers of Satan. Satan and his followers had warred in heaven against the 2/3rd majority who chose Jesus as their future savior.

An estimated number of 109+ billion came up to the present time with additional daily births estimated at 16,000/hr or 140.16 million/yr.

If we take 1/2 of the 109+ billion mortals as 1/3rd (Satan's Crew) of the total = 54.5 Billion and add it we get a total of 163.5 Billion.

Then take 1/2 of 140.16 million yearly births (Satan's Crew) =70.08 million and add it to the pre-existent total we get an additional 210.24 million.

Then project it another 50 years into the future without increasing it forever expanding births, we get 10.5 Billion to be added to the 163.5 Billion, resulting in 174.4 Billion Spirit Souls who were born on planet Kolob** to reside in future mortal bodies. [** Kolob is where God and his wives*** reside (*** see estimated numbers below).]

This number is required to be calculated as the full contingent of spirits who were convened in a council in Heaven voting between Jesus and Satan. [Remember these calculations are only good if the world ends in 50 years].

So 174.4 Billion spirit children (30 times larger than earth's present population) of God were assembled in the largest mass meeting ever held anywhere in the Cosmos!

While the size of that assembly is mind boggling, there are other issues , of creating that number equally as mind boggling.

Remember we have just one male God impregnating the mothers of those 174.4 Billion spirits. To estimate how many children per wife, we need some assumptions. Let's first assume 1,000 wives - 174,400,000.000 divided by 1, 0000 = 174,400,000 or 174.4 million per wife!

Assume 10,000 wives = 17,440,000 or 17.44 million per wife!

Assume 100,000 wives = 1,744,000 or 1.744 million per wife!

Assume 1,000,000 wives = 174,400 or 174.4 thousand per wife.

Assume 10,000,000 wives = 17,440 or 17.44 thousand per wife!

Assume 100,000,000 wives = 1,744 or 1.44 thousand per wife!

Assume 1,000,000,000 (one billion) wives = 174 per wife!

Assume 10,000,000,000 (ten Billion) wives = 17.4 per wife

Eternal Marriage? Eternal joyous sex?
Eternal Nonsense?

The absurdity of the phallic fantasy component of Mormon doctrine, a cornerstone of Mormonism, disqualifies its leaders and followers from any intellectual participation in the discussion and denial of civil rights to the gay community. If they can modify the absurdity to a believable platform, perhaps then they may thrust their collective conscience into the debate. However, in making such an adjustment, it will likely destroy the church which relies so heavily on temple marriage and baptism/salvation for the dead! Temples, the phallic icon of the church, will become obsolete in the process.

26

The Religious Empire: Public Enemy No. 1

March 11, 2009 at 22:43:08

The wars in Gaza, Afghanistan, Iraq and elsewhere have their root cause in the religious establishment. Likewise the war that rages around the globe against gays and lesbians has its roots in the religious establishment. We may look at symptoms of the empire as root causes for any conflict such as Hamas sending rockets into Israel or the Taliban fight against the UN or Shiite/Sunnis placed IEDs improvised explosive devices] blowing up American troops, but those are not root causes, mere symptoms.

I recently exchanged email with a coder in Bangladesh who informed me he could not work on developing a website concerning protection for gays and lesbians for me. Not only is homosexuality banned in Bangladesh, but apparently also thought and discussion about it. Homo-sexuality in Bangladesh or anywhere in the world is not of itself a root cause for governments to limit, restrict or ban such life style; it is the inherent power of the religious establishment.

We can discuss all of the problems of the world as extensively and completely as we wish but we will never get to the bottom (root) of the real issue until we are willing to take on the religious empire.

In 1887, the US Supreme court without argument or invited discussion declared by fiat that corporations were to be considered as persons under the constitution the same as naturally born citizens with all the rights and immunities afforded the natural born.

Prior to that time the same court held that the constitutional prohibition against the Congress (and by the 14th Amendment state legislatures), making laws respecting an establishment of religion applied to courts as well. Hence courts turn their back on justice.

In both cases, it would be absurd to think that a great deal of lobbying had not taken place privately with the court for it to enact such Orwellian doctrines. As a result, corporations have trampled on the rights of US citizens and courts have invalidated just causes for action by plaintiffs against religious organizations. Often there is little if any distinction between the two entities.

U.S. common law has its roots in English common law and with it the court of Chancery with its legal notions of equity which often infringes upon of the claimed rights of churches so that rights claimed by the citizenry as against the church are considered. For American courts to curtail equity at the door of the church is an abomination that needs to be dealt with.

As an example, in Vancouver, Washington in April 1976 I was summoned before a Stake President's Court (an inferior Mormon Church court) for priesthood insubordination (I had ordained a black man). At issue was my membership in the church. Upon arriving at the time and place designated, I filed with the head of that court, Orson Arnold, a complaint in the Melchezedek Priesthood Court of the church alleging illegal and criminal conduct on the part of leaders of the church as against the interests of members of the church formerly held in trust by the church president as trustee-in-trust. I told Mr. Arnold that under church court rules he must immediately terminate the trial and submit the complaint to the church leaders. Further, that it would be inequitable of him to proceed to remove my membership, thus my standing to sue, prior to the time that the church leaders stood trial on the charges of my complaint. [Church history recorded a similar trial held against church founder, Joseph Smith, Jr.]

Mr. Arnold threw the papers to the floor and ordered me to sit down. I reiterated my position at which point several members of the court attempted to place their hands on me to force me to sit down. I asked which of them wanted a lawsuit for false arrest. At that point they backed off and I left. Shortly after returning home a letter of excommunication previously prepared was served upon me. I took the position then and still do that any action by the local church court was illegal and inequitable so that in truth and fact the letter of excommunication was null and void.

In administrative law, all avenues of appeal must be exhausted before one can file a case in a court of law seeking redress. I filed a notice of trial de novo with the presidency of the church which was denied. [A trial de novo means a complete and new trial without consideration of the results of the first inferior trial. It is a matter of right from inferior civil courts to superior civil courts. It was also a matter of right within the legal procedure rules of the church court at the time.] Since the invalid act of the inferior court was left to stand in the view of the presidency of the church it remains invalid to this day.

Later I attempted to raise the issue of that standing within the purview of a civil court and was left hanging with the issue being non-justiciable by a civil court under the establishment clause. As a result, the church (in a generic sense) can get away with crimes and violations committed within its own protected paradigm.

Many such cases both in and out of the Mormon Church were brought to my attention as an attorney with a request from the victims for redress but sadly I was not able to help them because of the procedures I have cited. However as I write this one case comes to mind in which I feel I would be remiss if I didn't tell about it.

A medical doctor with years of practice and good standing within the Mormon Church wrote me a letter of appeal to help him. Both he and his wife had been excommunicated from the church a short while after they had relocated from Phoenix, AZ to Bountiful, UT [A Salt Lake City suburb]. Living in a densely populated Mormon community, the taint of excommunication was a financial disaster to him and he didn't deserve it [Mormons need church leaders authority to socialize with excommunicants without risk of excommunication themselves. My own nephew sought permission from his Stake president to communicate with me, his uncle, in order to prepare for a family reunion!]

The doctor's offense to the church was that he had allowed himself to be used as a medical examiner in viewing the body of John Singer as it was lying in a mortuary in Salt Lake City. The deceased, it appeared, had died from a shotgun blast in the back.

John Singer's picture had recently appeared on the front page of Newsweek magazine and a featured article about him discussed his fight with the state of Utah over the issue of his doing home education of his children. John was an excommunicated Mormon of the polygamous faction which was an embarrassment to the mainstream Mormon Church particularly after the publicity of the Newsweek article.

Apparently shortly before his death, Singer had gone down to his mail box on the highway and was confronted by Utah State/County law officers who attempted to serve papers on him regarding the legal fight he had ongoing with the state. As he turned to walk away one of the officers fired a shotgun blast at him killing him instantly.

Whether they were there to arrest him or only to serve papers is not the issue. He was not armed and was killed (murdered) by officers the state of Utah.

John's wife Vicky, [polygamists usually have one officially married wife and other wives are not official] requested the Mormon doctor to go to the mortuary and report to her the nature of her husband's death since she had not been allowed to view the body.

The basis of the summons given to the good doctor, challenging both he and his wife for their membership, was an allegation of "cavorting with known excommunicants". They were excommunicated and of course distressed at such an injustice. No civil court can or will intervene in such an injustice. Usually some dispersion is afterwards cast upon the moral character of the excommunicants to disguise the true reason for the action.

I do not pick out the Mormon Church as an exclusive entity violating the rights and commerce of individuals but only as an example of how absolute authority is corrupted by the religious empire.

The world-wide religious empire has far too strong a hold on the life and death of members of the public because of its safe and protected position as an exclusive imperialism. All other issues aside, this world will not progress to the freedom it needs until such time as the religious empire is dismantled!

Suggested Reading: The Religious Empire: An investigation of the religious empire in the United States 1975

By Martin A Larson & C. Stanley Lowell

Library of Congress Catalog No 75-27270

ISBN 0-88331-082-1

27

LEST OUR HEADS GET SWOLLEN, REMEMBER.........

October 13, 2011 at 09:00:51

ONE IN SEVEN/ BILLIONTH OF HUMANITY EQUALS ME, YOU OR ANY ONE OF US ON PLANET EARTH!

The old Swedish saying, "Ve get so soon old and yet so late schmart", certainly applies to me in my life. At the age of 82 plus it is sobering to stop and grasp the reality of how insignificant each of us are in relationship to the total mass of humanity treading this million plus year old planet.

In midlife I had my crisis as many males do realizing that I had just allowed myself to cruise along without any special effort to make a name for myself. One would have to say that is the course of life for the majority of humanity, live and let live.

Yet driving me in the dark recesses of my brain was some vague thought that I had some significant duty to perform for the God of my dreams. I couldn't put my finger on it because it had happened like a burst of light and then fading into grey and mystery within moments, months and years so that by the time of my midlife crises I could only remember I had spoken to some image of an otherworldly dimension.

Unfortunately for me I was raised Mormon and I learned that God can call one to a mission in this life. A calling of one life out of those 7.0 billion lives performing a function primarily for the benefit or protection of those 7.0 billion others. Such a thought would be a burden to the mind if believed and I was trained to believe.

Predestination is a term used to explain the roles many of us in making a mark in this world like Steven Jobs whom we recently lost. Did he have any specific precognitive concept of his goal in life? I don't know, perhaps he did. If he didn't then his contribution to the progress of the world was a natural outgrowth of his intelligence and curiosity. That is to say he didn't have the burden of a belief that he had some mission to fulfill. What propelled him? Was it in the idea of fame or fortune as drives so many among us?

Unlike predestination, the Mormon concept of a directed life, that is a life directed by other-worldly sources, is called fore-ordination. That is, that one is fore-ordained of God to perform some function in life which she or he has a calling to do but which she or he may choose not to do as an act of free agency. Yet the "knowing" of a call to mission especially when it is in the foggy recesses of the brain can become a burden to the one called. Keeping in mind the one in seven point zero billionth percentages of humanity and one's personal insignificance is a challenge.

At age twenty I was called to a mission in the UK by George Albert Smith then president of the Mormon Church.   I served two years but unlike most missionaries I was called to a temporal mission in acting as the Mission architect providing meeting facilities for some dozen or so branches of the church. Most significant was the participation in the change of mindset to expand the temple presence of the church outside the western hemisphere by doing the initial legwork for the London Temple in 1951. I kept the secret but little did I know that issue would burden me in later life. In fact it was later discovered to be in contradiction of the deeply embedded sense of mission that had bugged me for some dozen years by that time.

A wife and five children later in 1966, my sense of crisis blossomed and I sought some credential by which I would be accepted in performing that sense of mission which I still had no recollection of. Later as a credentialed attorney, on April 2, 1976 I shook the church with the public ordination of a young black man to forbidden priesthood. That was a struggled decision which I made after five years of seeking counsel of church leaders which was denied me so I was left with my own conscience to act upon. Shortly after this I gained a recall of that fuzzy otherworldly "event" which then set me in opposition to most of what Mormonism stands for.

A couple of years later the church reversed itself on forbidden black priesthood by seeking "worthy" black male members to ordain. I had been given to understand that the main meat of my mission was to act to prevent the coup d'état of the church in capturing control of the government of the United States and later of the world viz-a-viz the military might of the U.S. thereby establishing it's concept of the "Kingdom of God" on earth with the church leader as earth "king".

Since 1968 when Mormon George Romney, Mitt's father, ran for president I have been faced with the realization that the Mormon coup d'état which my fuzzy experience taught me was to be stopped or curtailed is an ever present danger in our society.

At age 82, I am seeing and feeling those signs of aging which bother me and cause me to want to pass off on my sense of foreordained mission. There are others out there with younger minds who can do a better job. I know they exist by other-worldly info. You can all simply come together by contacting me at director@americans-united-against-fascist-and-theocratic-governmnet.org and making yourselves known. I will then put you together to accomplish this. One need not be anti-Mormon, simply anti-fascist and anti-theocratic.

28

LABELS: MOSLEM, CHRISTIAN, JEW

December 8, 2009 at 09:27:14

Why argue, ye religious men,

Which God or gods, or where or when,

He spoke, or they, their words again?

What matters:"Does the good remain?"

Do labels: Moslem, Christian, Jew

Make any difference? All are true

To those who believe. The will to do;

That tells the tale the whole world through.

The heart is where the truth begins;

Where faith that conquers hate and wins

Against all odds. What more to ask

Than being partners in that task?

The wisdom of the past is here.

Its message comes both loud and clear:

"True brotherhood is for all men,

To state that truth with tongue and pen."

The One or Ones who hold the sky,

Who live on earth, who reign on high;

Do they care whether black or white,

if in our souls, or hearts are right?

'Tis love of self and neighbor, too,

That tells the story, straight and true.

The labels, Moslem, Christian, Jew,

Mean naught unless God's work we do.

John W. Fitzgerald. Ed. D (ret.)
Chaplain (Major) Utah N.G. (ret.)
19 July 1976

John Fitzgerald was a friend and mentor of mine. He spent an hour every day of his retirement writing at least one poem about the things that were the closest to him. Love, family, friends and the world's inhabitants.

He passed in late 1998 at the age of 95. His outspoken love of fellow man regardless of skin color or ethnic sculpturing cost him his membership in the Mormon Church when he attempted to reason with authority within the racist regime.

I attended his funeral services in a commercial wedding chapel in South Salt lake City because he was shunned from hundreds of LDS chapels at death by the church he had attempted to reason with.

I stood at the microphone left open after a closing prayer and a ceremony which attempted to whitewash away the greatness of that man.

"A hero", I said,"is a man who does something that needs to be done; at a time when it needs to be done; that no one else will do. John I salute you! You are my hero!"

I added, "For those present who know what I reference, I need say nothing more"

Leaving the podium I was spun around and cursed for being present at what had been advertised as an open service honoring the man for the greatness of his life and the goodness he had shed as a life time educator along the Wasatch Front of Utah.

So even in death, before his remains had been interred, he was insulted by the ignorance of his own family who had placed his body in a white Panama suit to emulate the white burial trappings of a Mormon Elder which his excommunication for intell-ectual Integrity deprived him of.

I ran across John's poem today while reminiscing the things he and I shared over 30 years ago.

I weigh the wisdom in that poem as against the lack of long term wisdom on the part of President Obama in deciding to make a surge in the war in Afghanistan.

Continuing the eight year old war with more troops, munitions and tactical weapons flies completely in the face of the God we mouth a belief in.

The Reagan concept of maintaining peace through strength AKA intimidation is completely the opposite of what is needed. Peace comes only by way of negotiation, adjustment and compromise.

This is a lesson Barack Obama and his tiered advisers have never had.

The John W. Fitzgerald papers were donated to Utah State University Libraries and can be scanned here:

http://library.usu.edu/specol/manuscript/collms102.html

29

A NEW YEAR'S RESOLUTION FOR ALL AMERICANS

January 2, 2010 at 16:58:03

I have lived for eighty years and am still waiting for Americans to rise to their obligations under the Constitution to take the helm to run the government both federal and state.

Sorry folks but it is time to stop wishing, and start doing something affirmative by breaking up the political quagmire in Washington. There are a number of things we the voters can do to turn our seemingly irreversible situation around. We must first come to grips with the fact that our political and economic future can no longer be entrusted to politicians who feather their own nest at the expense of the electorate/taxpayer.

At present our national debt is hovering around 14 trillion dollars, not counting the long term obligations of government, in paying for social benefits over the long term. We are in a state of bankruptcy and no additional bailouts of worthless paper money will help us.

While the Constitution prohibits any litmus test for candidates for public office, that applies to the making of any laws which would set those tests. We the people have the unencumbered right to select and vote for candidates who meet our own notion of exactly what a good candidate for public office should stand for and we can enforce it at the ballot box.

We have been deceived that we have a two party system. What we have is a one party system with different engravings on each side of the coin, which makes it a dictatorship.

There are a number of things we have observed over the years that have helped bring the country to where it is. The first and foremost would be the organized misinformation which we all were subjected to in the public school system. That would be the false history of the development of the United States. Guns, gunpowder, cannons and the saber, not God, created the United States from the Atlantic to the Pacific. The same deception began the expansion of the influence of the U.S. to where today it is has bases in foreign countries by the hundreds to maintain its intimidating influence for the benefit of the elite all paid for by the taxpayers.

Communism was not defeated by democracy but rather by capitalism at the expense of America's workers. The reward for supporting that effort has resulted in the elite moving jobs offshore to where our workers have nothing more than rampant unemployment and all the pain that it portends. That maneuver has been called protecting America's vital interests with war, hype and propaganda to get the worker to side with the wealthy in supporting war against created enemies further destroying our homeland from within. We need to wake up and not rely on some messiah appearing in the sky to save us. WE MUST DO IT OURSELVES! IT IS SIMPLE BUT WILL REQUIRE OUR COMMITMENT BEGINNING RIGHT NOW! A NEW DECADE OF RESOLUTION!

As a first step I believe that the majority among us have no real idea of how all this has happened. I suggest that every adult American obtain and read a copy of Professor Howard Zinn's Book, <u>A People's History of the United States</u>. By reading it we can all come to a common understanding of where we are and how we got here. Only two million copies have been sold world-wide and we need at least ten million people to read it to shake off the shackles that inhibit us. We can also educate ourselves somewhat by watching the documentary film, THE PEOPLE SPEAK made from the book. That DVD will be available for purchase this January and was shown on the History Channel this past Month.

After reading it we need to organize***ourselves to accomplish the following suggestions:

1. Remove from office any member of the House of Representatives who has already served three terms.

2. Remove all Senators who have served two terms.

3. Limit the wealthy from office. Annual income of over $500,000.00 the last three years will disqualify any candidate. Personal assets of more than ten million Dollars will also disqualify. We need a congress truly representative of the masses.

5. If a candidate for public office refuses to enter into a contract with his or her constituents to comply with promises contractually made to those constituents, he or she shall not be voted for. If he or she has made any such contract and upon election there after fails to perform; he or she shall be subject to immediate removal from office for breach of contract. No more of this bait and switch BS.

6. Every candidate for public office will promise on penalty of perjury and breach of contract that he or she will make every effort to terminate the Federal Reserve System Law and return the printing of money to the government of the masses of people. This law is up for renewal in 2012! It is a law by which the elite have toyed with us too long!

These are litmus tests which we the voter can enforce at the ballot box.

NOW THIS IS JUST A START!

30

SOCIALISM IS ABOUT PEOPLE: FASCISM IS ABOUT CORPORATIONS

September 21, 2009 at 03:44:56

I for one am appalled at the spectacular event that happened at Capitol Hill in Washington D.C. this past weekend.

The picture shows thousands of protestors of the Obama Administration holding placards; some depicting him as Adolph Hitler others with icons of a monkey! The group seems to have been deceived into believing that the economic situation in the country is the fault of Obama. Nothing could be further from the truth! He inherited the financial ruins of the Bush/Cheney years and is attempting the impossible task of putting Humpty-Dumpty back together again!

I have since learned that Mormon Glenn Beck was the instigator of that mass gathering. The fact that

Glenn Beck spouts off extreme right wing inflammatory rhetoric similar to that of Rush Limbaugh, supports my allegations in past articles that while the Mormon Church ostensibly abandoned racism when it caved into my pressure against their position in 1978 concerning Black priesthood, that racism is still deeply embedded in the Mormon psyche.

Social segregation is still practiced at Brigham Young University. And the Genesis Group of Black men within the Mormon Church continues to exist to gain communion not shared with racist Mormons.

It would be appropriate that the Mormon Church censure Beck or at least make a public statement rebuking any vestiges of racism within the church. It would be most appropriate that they publicly work to snuff out those vestiges among their own congregations!

I would estimate that if one could have walked among that crowd and solicited an identity as to religious affiliation that at least three fourths of them would claim to be Christian!

Yet they cannot be Christian or they would know for a fact that the first organization of Christianity under the Apostle Peter was a communistic society for, "they had all things in common." "Things" meaning property which they shared equally. (Acts 4:22) If one reads the entire chapter it would appear as though God wanted that commitment out of the early church for he put to death a husband and wife who lied to Peter about having consecrated their all to the Christian Commune. Either that is true or the Gospel writer is a liar!

The boasted claims of the historical past of democracy winning over Communism in regards to the Soviet Union's collapse is a complete lie for it was not democracy but capitalism that won the struggle. Not only did capitalism win against Communism, but it made damn sure that the cost of winning was applied against the wealth and freedom of Americans by placing a humongous debt on American Taxpayers as the price for the delusion.

Corporate greed has no conscience whatever!

Corporate capitalism is a dictatorship that regards humans as a dispensable resource commodity which it manipulates to achieve its bottom line profits. If it could totally manufacture products and deliver services with robots it would have no conscience whatever if unemployment were 25% of the population as long as it could make a profit (not likely)!

Strange that Capitalism in the form of Insurance-Corporate Greed can organize so many people to show up and participate in a gathering in opposition to the interests and welfare of other people including themselves. One can only deduce that those people are not only ignorant but have the intellectual capacity of robots programmed to self destruct!

What could only be worse was if all those people spent their own money making the trip to Washington with all that implies to demonstrate against their own personal "Christian" ethics.

To confuse Adolph Hitler with Socialism is the height of ignorance; He was a fascist corporate-loving monster with a hatred for communism (socialism).

Some examples of socialism in our country that work are:

The military and national guard

Police

Prosecutors

Courts and judges

City or community water resources

Municipal waste disposal

National, City and county administrations

County Health departments

Port authorities both water and air

Medicaid

Medicare

Workers compensation

Unemployment compensation

Social Security

To argue that a taxpayer's money is going to some use that he or she disapproves of is utterly useless since the tax when paid belongs to the taxing authority and its pool of duly lawful obligations created by legislation.

If the protestors want to change things then they should dump out of office all incumbents and replace them with new faces with a mandate at the next election. It isn't going to faze any of them by a march to Washington!

If six hundred thousand or a million people want to assemble in protest in Washington D.C they should do so at the door of the Federal Reserve and demand the Congress terminate the Federal Reserve in 2012 when its authority expires. Then follow up by requiring the US Treasury to mint and print money of the people and ending interest compounded or simple on any obligations of the government.

Most Americans are not aware that the Federal Reserve is not Federal but private and that it was created by a conspiracy of foreign bankers on Jekyll Island off North Carolina and put into effect not by the Congress but by President Woodrow Wilson during a recess of the congress in December 1912.

And further, that the sixteenth amendment (income Tax) was created afterwards (1913) to overcome the

1895 Supreme Court decision outlawing income tax as direct tax in violation of the Constitution. Only in this way could the government pay the obligations borrowed from the Federal Reserve by notes or Bonds.

The money borrowed was worthless having nothing of value to back it up except for the power of the government to confiscate the wealth of the people through taxation. This was an abominable act of fascist control of the finances of the United States and it has had control for 98 years! Where are the masses protesting this travesty upon the taxpayer? So all masses of protestors as described above are missing the point; they are protesting symptoms of the problem not its source!

If you robots of Corporate Greed want to protest; make your voices heard in the next two years at your local state and national elections by voting out every incumbent with over two terms experience.

Another thought.... Everyone wants to go to "Heaven" or so they think. But why would they want to do that when it is a social scene from start to finish. So then why not practice for it in this life????

31

WORLD PEACE IS IMPOSSIBLE WITHOUT SPIRITUAL ALIGNMENT

June 4, 2009 at 23:30:34

President Obama gave a speech in Cairo in which he talked of a new beginning between America and Islam. He spoke of democracy and women's rights. All the talk of bringing those two elements of America's view into the lifestyle of Muslims is diametrically opposed to Islam's Sharia law.

No person or group of persons will or are able to make such drastically opposed changes to basic belief systems without the trauma of a crushing disintegration of all that is held dear to the mind and "heart".

The primitive brain of man known as the reptilian brain is coupled with the limbic system. It is there that basic elements of eating, sleeping, reproduction, fear, anger, fight, flight, and emotionally blocking new ideas running counter to what has been programmed over the years in the belief system. Any new understanding entering the "Gray" matter is controlled by the initial biases of the Limbic system. It is a gate keeper. Yogi Berra said, "There are some people if they don't already know, you can't tell them". That is why habits or belief systems are hard if not impossible to break.

Jews have it and so do Christians and Muslims along with all other humans of varied beliefs. In contemporary lingo it is called being brainwashed. Thus all devout believers of those religions addressed by Obama are brainwashed to several but each a unique and variant belief system.

The messages of Obama which deviate from beliefs of Muslims simply pass through the ears of Muslims like water off a "ducks back"! The same can be said for his speech which threatens the notions of Jews with respect to the "Holy Land"; notions that have been programmed into the minds of Jews for centuries. Likewise any part of his speech which challenges radical Christian belief systems also falls off their ears. In the end, each group can only envision peace if the other two groups yield to the programming of a single group. It would be like having two joker cards in a single hand!

It is ignorant nonsense to make such a speech for peace while ignoring the realities of human consciousness with its deep seated biases.

A history of the world, particularly the Middle East is riddled with religious notions of which belief system is correct and should prevail over mankind. The truth is that no religion can prove with empirical evidence that it is correct to the point of overcoming any observable objection to it. That is to say that no religion can prove beyond any reasonable doubt that it is true. Faith in an un-provable notion will never make it true no matter how long the belief system has existed.

Reducing family legends to a written document cannot make it any truer than it was at the outset. All three of the major religions discussed here have their roots in the Abraham oral tradition until a character named Moses reduced the legends to a written form as the book of Genesis. If there is any truth to the story, the truth would be that God approved the stealing of birth rights established under traditions of the ancestors of Abraham by driving the first born son of Abraham into the wilderness to steal for his second son, Isaac, the birthright promises of the first born, Ishmael.

This was followed up by Abraham's grandson Esau being deprived of his firstborn birthright by deception in giving it to second son Jacob or Israel. So the written story establishes the God of Abraham as approving liars and a cheats if such deception was, as appears, approved by Abraham's God. Without making any excuses or rationalizations how does that square with a reasonable person's concept of a just and loving God?

As to which descendants of Abraham have the birthright promises of custom, a court of law would have to rule that the descendants of Ishmael are the legal heirs and they happen to be Arabs. So the belief by Jews that by God's divine sanction they are rightful heirs to Jerusalem no matter which of their later kings or prophets made such an assertion is totally flawed. Again it does not matter how long the belief has been held or how many times it has been reduced to writing, the lands of the Middle East belong to Arabs under the inheritance laws of the ancestors of Abraham.

There has not been a case of mistaken identity as complete and flawed as the descendants of Judah upon who was bestowed an egotistic identity as God's special/chosen people as heirs to the promise of the scepter not "departing Judah or the lawgiver from between his feet until Shiloh come". The idea of combining the notions of Israel's God with racial purity/religion and right of governing the earth by Jews has been a con game of the millenniums. It has been a deception without parallel! Unfortunately millions of Jews have suffered death and abuse because of it.

The smarter ones of Israel, the ten tribes who departed and mixed their identity with other earthlings after the 70 year captivity in Babylon were obviously sick and tired of the false promises of Abraham's God and instead of returning to the Holy Land are reported to have gone north into Europe who's later descendants became Christians.

While the centuries old conflict between Arabs and Jews is well known, the major conflict came after the announcement by Mohammed that he had been caught up to converse with God-Allah. That announcement and the Koran which he wrote established in the minds of Arabs that they, not Jews, are the chosen of God and their destiny is to bring the entire world to Muslim acceptance of Allah along with its Sharia law which is in conflict with Judaism, Christianity, democracy and centuries of developed civil/human rights of men and women in particular.

Mohammed's story is no more empirically provable than is Abraham's but the former relies on the latter for credibility. Thus they both negate the other.

Christianity is sandwiched between Judaism and Islam both in time frames and in authority. The exception of Christianity is the claim that Jesus, a Jewish descendant of King David is the "made in the flesh" God of Jews, Muslims and Christians. While it attempts to exalt the notion of love and grace of God it has as much blood on its hands as either Judaism or Islam. Neither Judaism nor Islam take any stock in the Christ story other than perhaps admit to his being a prophet.

The bare bones truth is that not any one of the three major religions can reach to the degree of absolute certainty by which faith or trust in it can bring about a peaceful earth. That is to say that not any of its, separate or combined, thesis' rises to the level of certainty that killing another human soul over its beliefs, laws or rules can be justified by God or, more importantly, by the intelligence of man.

Instead of preaching peace and reconciliation to Muslims while backing the right of Israel with its stockpile of atom bombs to preemptively attack Iran to prevent any chance of Iran acquiring its own bomb for self protection, Mr. Obama needs to be addressing root causes of the ages old conflicts.

Seeking a consensus of purpose among them in a search to resolve these issues can only come about as a result of spiritual alignment from compromise. While that is not the arena of a democratic government under the U.S. Constitution, it can be referred to men and women who may by experience [not formal training as Doctors of Divinity] be prepared to address such issues outside of government.

While it cannot be true that all three divergent religious views are correct, it is indisputable that all three can be incorrect! There is a way in which the Cosmos can resolve these conflicts in bringing peace and co-existence to Arabs, Jews and Christians. We just need to reach out for it in earnest desire. This is an area where the Quantum Enigma [the "spooky stuff" of Einstein] can produce answers.

Does Mr. Obama have the wisdom and fortitude to properly initiate such a procedure?

Only time will tell! True and lasting peace awaits his affirmation of correct procedures

Painted from a dream of the author
symbolic of peace in Palestine

32

'In God We Trust': The Most Blasphemous Statement Ever Engraved

May 3, 2009 at 16:17:02

It is said that the Puritans landed at Plymouth Rock in November 1620. It is also said that because these "Christians" came to the new world to worship God according to the dictates of conscience, the persistent belief of ill informed charismatic's is that the United States was founded as a Christian nation and therefore we must declare to the world that in, "God we Trust." That belief is far off the mark!

PLYMOUTH ROCK picture Public Domain

225

From observation of history we can read that the government which was established by the Massachusetts Bay Company was not Christian but rather Mosaic. The "Body of Liberties" of 1641 stated that "If any man after legal conviction shall have worshiped any other god, but the lord god (?), he shall be put to death." Death was also prescribed for witchcraft, blasphemy, murder, sodomy, homosexuality, adultery, and kidnapping. Old Testament texts were literally copied into the New England law.

It was there that a bounty was placed upon the head of Native Americans by a payment of 12 (English) pounds for his or her scalp*. That was later raised to 100 pounds. Bounty hunters flourished and natives perished! It was there at Salem that the witch hunts [more bounty hunting] and executions by burning were carried out. The law was more like the Muslim Sharia law of Theocratic totalitarianism than Christian. (See: The Search for Christian America, pp. 28-35.)

Just seventeen years after Plymouth Rock, in the early morning hours of May 26, 1637, believing themselves to be directed by God. An armed group under the command of John Mason stealthily entered the compound of the Pequot Indian tribe and set the huts on fire then shooting anyone, men, women or children attempting to escape the flames. Those of the tribe that they did not kill that day they finished off later on July 14th. **"God laughed his Enemies and the Enemies of his People to Scorn, making**

them as a fiery Oven ... Thus did the Lord judge among the Heathen, filling the Place with dead Bodies" (Segal and Stienback, Puritans, Indians, and Manifest Destiny, pp. 111-112, 134-135).

Parts of the foregoing are paraphrased from Biblical Discernment Ministries - 6/98

Puritans had the notion that they were God's special people and that they were establishing a new "Zion". It was in fact the beginning of the diabolical doctrine of "Manifest Destiny" which nearly two centuries later re-spawned the notions of two New Englanders, Joseph Smith, Jr. and Brigham Young with their Old Testament/Muslim notions about Polygamy and totalitarian theocracy hiding behind a facade of Jesus Christ.

With this mindset of a special calling from God, the puritan fathers of America stole the land of the Indians and if they could not convert them to Christ they would slaughter them and even if converted were still discriminated against.

For more info on the savagery of the Puritans see: NEW ENGLAND FRONTIER: Puritans and Indians 1620-1675 by Alden T. Vaughan. 1965 (Little Brown & Company, Boston/Toronto), revised 1995

We see from conduct of later generations even after the Revolutionary and Civil Wars, the idea of Manifest Destiny continued among American leaders with continued slaughter of Indians and theft of their land. 321 treaties of peace by Indians with the US government were broken by the government. Native Americans who survived the American Holocaust were herded like cattle onto reservations that "Christian" Americans deemed worthless land [The Jewish Holocaust had a precedent in America for Hitler to follow].

Indeed the evil concept of Manifest Destiny still lurks today in the shadows of our national leaders spurred on by such diatribe as found in the Bush agenda of the Project for the New American Century [PNAC] Sept., 2000]. Even our current leadership has no apparent thought of backing off it!

IN GOD WE TRUST? WHO'S GOD? WHAT GOD? The war mongering God of the Old Testament; the "peaceful" God of the New Testament; the totalitarian God of the Koran?

IN GOD WE TRUST? For what purpose? That our mistaken belief the United States is God's Chosen warrior to subdue all other cultures into submission by superior weapons inventiveness, inventory and deception? That the pilgrim's pride of Manifest Destiny is not a delusion of evil proportions?

Ever since "Christians" invaded the Americas, land/resource theft, massacre, genocide, and mind control by a different religious indoctrination has reduced the former natives of the land to servitude or suicide. Suicide by Canadian Indians is reported to be the highest per-capita rate in the world followed by American Indians. Today only 2.5% remains of the populations existing at the time of the conquistadors. What European's guns did not destroy their diseases did!

DNA proves the ancestors of the North and South American Indians migrated over the Bering land bridge from Siberia twelve to fourteen thousand years ago some six to eight thousand years before the time frames of the Adam and Eve myth spawning the malignant traditions of Judaism, Christianity and Islam by which war and slaughter of human's under any supposed guise or by repressive sanctions was given "God's" approval!

We Americans have supported administrations that have deceived and betrayed us. From Andrew Jackson's genocidal behavior in killing eight Hundred native Americans and allowing his troops to mutilate the dead bodies; his driving tribes such as the Christian converted Cherokees off their ancestral lands in mid winter with 50% mortality: the military incursion into Mexico to steal the territory of ten western states; The wars against the Indians to steal ancestral lands; the false flag operation of "Remember the Maine"; the infamy of killing 3,000 military at Pearl harbor; the false flag operation of 9-11 killing another 3,000 to control mid-east oil and aid and abet the establishment of Israel; building and using the A-bomb not once but twice along with the refusal to rule out first strike use of the 3,000 stockpile against any enemy; maintaining in excess of 600 military bases throughout the world to suppress the independence of other nations; spending more money each year on military/industrial adventures than all other nations combined; using torture not to achieve security for Americans but to cover up the conspiratorial conduct of a past administration!

The list could go on ad-infinitum!

"In God we Trust" to forgive us these offenses? No! We have to first admit our crimes against humanity; feel sorry and ask forgiveness!

America needs to repent and to confess our sins to the world and ask its forgiveness before God can or will forgive us.

We need to gain some humility by backing off the course of Manifest Destiny. It will be good for America and the world.

We could start by changing the engraving on coin and currency to, "God forgive us", back off all future war games and close our military outposts.

Then and only then can we think in our hearts and show by our actions that, "In God we Trust"! And that God in whom we trust would be the true God of peace who predates by eons the mythical war mongering god of Abraham, Moses, Christ and Mohammed!

*scalping was not in vogue among the native tribes until the British and the Dutch used it as a trophy of war.

33

The Lincoln-Douglas Debates and the Mormon Cancer Waiting on Mitt Romney

May18, 2012 2:47 PM

Abraham Lincoln and Stephen A. Douglas were Illinois political rivals for a period of years prior to Lincoln being elected to the Presidency. In fact Lincoln agreed to serve just one term in the U.S House of Representatives to allow Douglas to be elected in the following term. Both were lawyers and Douglas a "back woods" judge.

Mormon lore is circulated in order to keep the members hyped up to the truth of their belief systems by assuring that church Founder Joseph Smith was indeed a prophet of God. So the following story is circulated.

According to legend, Smith is supposed to have told Douglas the following, "Mr. Douglas, the day will come when you will aspire to the presidency of the United States! Should you at any time speak adversely of the Mormon people, you will lose the election."

Smith, at the time, was himself a fugitive from justice in Missouri now leading his flock of Mormon converts who had traversed the Mississippi River from Missouri to Illinois as an agreed settlement of a war denominated as the "Missouri War".

Earlier, Smith as a prisoner had been allowed to escape while close to the Mississippi River while in transit to a change of venue for a trial on charges of sedition. His incarceration was the result of the war in which the church militia had capitulated to the National Guard troops of Missouri.

Since Smith died in the evening of June 27, 1844 from a hail of gunfire from his enemies at the Carthage, Ill. Jail, The claimed Douglas prophecy would have been made between the time of his rejoining his followers in Nauvoo, Illinois early in the 1840's and his death. His death was also shortly after he had declared his candidacy for president and had been crowned "Earth King" by his followers.

The church lore, whether accurate or not; and I never researched it, suggests that during one of the political debates between Douglas and Lincoln, the question was asked of both candidates what, if elected president, they would do with reference to the then apparently well known, "Mormon Problem".

Douglas answered that he would treat the problem like a doctor treats cancer, he would cut it out.

Lincoln answered that he would treat the problem like a farmer treats a large boulder in his fields, simply plow around it. Since Lincoln won election and Douglas lost, the fact of his allegedly speaking adversely of Mormons meant that Joseph Smiths's "prophecy" was true and he was a proven, prophet.

Well it makes for a good story to the gullible if in fact it ever was a timed reality not some tale made up after the fact as are so many of Smith's prophecies.

In reality, as we look at the ever encompassing Mormon deception spreading around the world like a cancer, it would appear as though Douglas had it right and Lincoln had it wrong.

Problem though, even if Douglas had it right there was no way as president of his acting to cut out the cancer unless he skillfully had diagnosed the real cancer i.e. quest for political empire hiding in a package of religion as a non religious event not otherwise proscribed by the First Amendment. Today with church membership now greater outside of the United States than it is within, it would be even more difficult but not impossible.

And the other problem facing a president even if Douglas had succeeded in winning election to the presidency is that he would be barred from surgically removing it since the non religious protected [political] aspects of Mormonism demonstrated in

Missouri and Illinois had yet to become a full bloom example as it did later in the Utah territory prior to statehood before and after the Lincoln-Douglas debates.

As recorded history of the United States shows, there are two Mormon related legal exceptions from Article VI clause 4 and the first Amendment that have set legal precedent. The first was the 1857 [before Lincoln's Presidency] march into Mormon country [Utah] by Johnston's army ordered to put down the Mormon political rebellion a mere ten years after leader Brigham Young led his followers to what would become the Utah Territory. And still later, The 1878 Supreme court ruling [Reynolds v U.S.] that since polygamy was not considered a Western custom and therefore then illegal by enacted law in the territory even though it was practiced as a claimed religious principle. In both instances the church submitted by officially suspending its political quest for empire and issuing the 1890 "manifesto" declaring polygamy was not to be practiced any longer as a religious principle; the immediate benefit of the Manifesto being the re-acquisition of property which had been escheated by the Government.

Gaining statehood and independence from territorial status of Utah was important to the church as it could still ride herd on the laws passed and enforced [or ignored] with statehood [free of congressional oversight as a territory] as it did prior to the 1857 Utah War and it could go underground with its agendas. Patience has to be observed as one of the enduring "virtues" of the Mormon Church leadership, faked patriotism notwithstanding.

The Reed Smoot Senate Hearings were held in Washington D. C. concerning the seating of Reed Smoot as the first Senator from Utah after Utah gained statehood before the turn of the twentieth century, the U. S. senate held up the seating of Smoot to make sure the church had submitted to the law outlawing polygamy.

Church President Joseph F. Smith was summoned twice over a two year period of time as a witness. At the second summons when questioned about the fact that He, Smith, had additional children by plural wives between the two summonses in spite of the fact that Utah had by then made polygamy a crime, the church president said," I'll take my chances with the law". It goes without saying that the church president is above the law in the Utah community. Attorneys who have sought to subpoena the "prophet" into court have learned how difficult, if not impossible, it is.

A couple of years ago, I had the opportunity to see the cover of the church magazine, the Ensign, which displayed on its cover the picture of two young African male missionaries happily carrying their Book of Mormons out to visit fellow countrymen selling Mormonism to the gullible.

Initially, the church missionary program was criticized by established Christian churches because the church only targeted Christians as potential converts. That is to say that the hard work done by the Christian community in bringing souls to Christ was being perverted by Mormon missionaries.

It was and still is easier to seek out converts from people who already had a belief in Christ than it was from non believers who had to be first converted to Christ.

If the church is using its black missionaries to convert other black Christians then the tact would be the same as it always had been i.e., stealing Christians from other Christian churches.

In any event, the Mormon effort is akin to a cancerous parasitical corruption of the traditional Christian community in matters of religion. It is also a parasitical corruption of democracy with an agenda to replace the Republic with a fascist dictatorial theocracy.

In order to accomplish that task, invention was at the root of the cancer. Invention of another bible [book of Mormon] as a lauded second witness to Christ; invention of a literal spiritual childhood of earth's peoples with a pre-existence in "heaven" all sexually fathered by a single immortal God; invention of a male dominated priesthood purportedly representing God; invention of a non-Christian yet claimed real Christian concept of polygamy; invention of an ultimate immortal destination to a celestial kingdom with eternal [endless] sex with plural wives pre-sealed in earthly temples; invention of the concept of becoming immortal gods in a literal sense having the job of amassing elements to create additional universes to lord over, control and populate with civilizations of mortal people whose souls [spirits] had been created by their god's polygamous sexual intercourse in an otherworldly pre-existent life.

All of this appeals to the genital areas of converted male Mormons [just thinking about it is a phallic experience]. It is this corrupted [cancerous] concept of Christianity that the church uses as a vehicle for success in slowly gaining members from traditional Christian Faiths.

It can be said that Stephen A. Douglas called it correctly as a "cancer" [whether in debate or otherwise] that needed to be excised. Lincoln on the other hand failed to recognize it for what it was and would simply ignore it allowing it to grow [as it has] to the point of near no return where we find it today. So much for Lincoln's foresight.

Yet there is a more sinister aspect of the cancer. It is a cancer of the body politic. It is a cancer that would surreptitiously invade the body politic of the United States gaining acceptance by deception of being true patriotic Americans and yet quietly in the middle of the night strip away freedoms from every man woman and child in the United States replacing it with a hard lined theocracy of "our way or no way"

At this point in history the US government is foolishly building a giant intelligence facility in the Utah desert which will record the heart beat, the spoken word and the mindset of everyone on the planet channeled into that facility for the Mormon Church to use to preemptively suppress any thought of resistance to its empire quest should Romney take the oath as president in January 2013; timely coinciding with completion of that spy facility.

That would be the crossing of the abyss [Rubicon] feared by Senator Frank Church in 1976 as the crossing from which there is no return!

Goodbye Miss American Pie! *Note! This article brought about a comment by a Mormon who called it an astonishing display of ignorance as the debate on the subject never happened between Lincoln and Douglas. My response was that the story was priesthood lore and that his comment was meant to smoke over the real issue of Mormon cancer of Christianity and political enterprise.*

34

ORGANIZED RELIGION: HIJACKING RIGHTS OF HUMANS

January 11.2009 at 11:50:54

Once upon a time, during the First Stone Age some 200,000 to 300,000 years ago, primitive man lived by a simple code. Smack someone and you get smacked back. Steal from someone and they will steal back. It was kind of a self ad-justifying order of justice.

The point is that behavior was controlled by a learned sense of knowing what the consequences for a particular action might be. People lived and died under that code. Obviously kind deeds attracted its own as well so that most people by the time they were adults pretty well knew how to live their lives and experienced the consequences of good or bad behavior on the spot. While tribal codes were imposed, there was no deferred judgment of penalties or rewards to consider that would be imposed after death to hinder or condition behavior in the present life.

Special individuals developed within the tribes who seemed to have particular abilities to heal and to spiritually guide members of the tribe. These were called Shamans and most primitive tribes had them. Often, these shamans were men who at an early age became aware of their own sexual orientation in which they tended toward the association of women. That decision was generally supported by the tribes and particularly the family. They were special and revered. Often they were go-betweens of male and female disputes. While the masculine male was a hunter warrior, females were food gatherers. The shamans would dress like and participate in female activities. Weaving, beadwork, food gathering and cooking were activities they excelled in.

In the ancient Americas, these individuals were what today we call "gay". In North America after European discovery, these individuals were called "Berdaches" (French) by Europeans. Their influence was noted among most of the Indian tribes. While they had male genitals, they loathed to have sexual contact with females, but rather became lovers for other males. Similar trends were observed in South America, Pacific Islands, Australian Aboriginals, Japan and elsewhere. The same conditions were known in Africa, Greece, Rome and even Europe.

Is indisputable that male homosexuality existed in all areas of the world prior to Christianization. Homosexuality was acknowledged and accepted as a part of normal human life. Lesbianism or female homosexuality was a con-current anomaly of tribal life as well. It flourished in ancient polygamous societies where there were large harems and insufficient sexual attention was given to individual wives. In most of these cases lesbianism was a condition of the situation as is prison homosexuality rather than the inborn gender of the individual. Yet an inborn gender trait was often considered the real gender rather than the genitals. Other forms of homosexuality existed in which the younger male partner was used to avoid pregnancy and family responsibility which often was deferred to a later time. In most cases these were not the result of inborn gender but rather a choice occasioned for other reasons. There clearly were abuses.

Nevertheless, the ancient code prevailed and there was little if any repercussion arising out of what was a customary practice openly known and lived. A person's body was his/her own to do with as wished. This was true in societies outside of the influence of organized religion.

In the European colonization of the world such as the Western Hemisphere, India, Africa and elsewhere, the invader brought with it its own moral code fashioned out of the Bible. In doing this these colonial governments sat in judgment of ages old lifestyle practices of natives they had conquered. Because those practices were deemed to be below the dignity and morality of European Christians they were suppressed.

South American conquests were accompanied by the priests of the Catholic Church imposing Catholicism on the Natives. Where the new code ordered death or beatings for practices of homosexuality, the Colonial Courts ordered it. This attitude caused the practice of homosexuality to be driven underground in the lives of those conquered. Nowhere to this day has homosexuality been defeated and destroyed by organized religion. Yet it has suffered abuse and discrimination by religious biased governments and main stream heterosexuals and even by closeted homosexuals.

In addition to physical pain, suffering and death imposed on homosexuals by governments, the influence of organized religion has added a burden of judgment of the homosexual as a sinner facing judgment from God in an afterlife.

The simplistic concept of Black vs. White, God vs. Satan which drives religion, is the deciding factor in what a member of society may think or do. In this, religion has inserted itself into the mind and body of individuals it wishes to control. Using fear it has hijacked the freedom of gullible followers by insisting it and only it has authority to speak for God and thus justifiably condemn practices it deems dirty and ungodly.

Unfortunately, we cannot realistically discuss the issue of homosexuality without making a judgment call on the authenticity of the Bible. The general reverence given to the Bible is that it is the inspired word of God (Mormons say as far as it is translated correctly). Many well meaning people repeat the standard reverence without thinking.

IT IS TIME FOR REAL WORLD!

The bible was written and compiled by men not God. The best that can be said about the Bible which is a compilation of numerous ancient books is that they were written by men. These writers at times attempted to place in the mouth of God, words which they them-selves thought God ought to utter according to their unique biases. Nowhere in the scriptures is there a word or statement directly from God.

NOWHERE!! I repeat NOWHERE!

Reliance on the utterances of the word of God written by "inspired" men as per the Bible is based on faith not fact!

St Paul expressed a definition of faith as the, "substance of things hoped for; the evidence of things unseen". That statement would gain no traction whatever in a court of law.

That human beings are being tossed about between the fabricated opposite poles of heaven and hell, is a situation designed by and for the benefit of the priestly class. From time immemorial that class has taken upon itself the right to guide the poor unsuspecting soul toward heaven's ambiguous salvation. It is and has always been a money making/prestige garnering/mind controlling occupation. Its key to success is promulgating fear! Of course the Bible has been kept and preserved for centuries! Why? Qui bono!

Let's take a common sense approach to the issue of sin. The worst that can be said about sinning is that any conduct classified as a sin by men pretending to speak for God is merely non-progressive/non benefiting conduct and becomes its very own reward or punishment.

Man may beat torture and kill others as punishment for offenses perceived as sin, but God doesn't punish for there is no need nor is it in the capacity of God. One may flunk a college exam but the reason for flunking is not a sin merely a deficiency. The punishment is in not obtaining the advantages that passing would have granted. However that is not the end as one can keep on trying until such time as the appreciation (and striving) for the benefits to be gained has outweighed the deficiency. It kind of equates with the idea of not putting pearls before swine (a matter of appreciation)!

In considering homosexual attitudes the same thing applies. On the part of the homosexual couples. The sin if there be any would be to choose a lifestyle (except as an inborn gender factor) that is not progressive (damning). But the sin would also be the reward if that was all you wanted to experience. The punishment would not be a spear that god would throw at you but rather the deprivation of some benefit that might have been gained by not having "sinned". Even then there is an opportunity to change (repent) at any time should one want to experience the other benefit such as heterosexual marriage and children. God has simply laid out the choices for actions to be chosen through free agency.

As to the inborn gendered homosexual, lesbian, bi-sexual and transvestite there is no sin in living your life in response to the natural sexual impulses. God would have to admit [res *ipsa loquitur (the thing speaks for itself)*] that somewhere in the cosmos things got a little skewed in DNA makeup and for this the cosmos is to blame if there be any blame! You have a God given right to live your life according to the dictates of conscience.

On the part of the anti gay individual: The sin is in the extension of hate toward an individual or individuals or conduct whom/which you have no appreciation for. The punishment and reward for hate is a deprivation of the experience of love and learning.

To the clergy: Your sin is your own damnation in failing to understand the love that God extends to those who exercise a right to free agency within the purview of His domain. You would rather order homosexual persons into a prison of the mind to be subject to your fear mongering tactics arising not out of love of or for God but rather your own fear of losing control over those you have usurped a right to dictate to in the name of God. Your reward and punishment is ignorance and blindness.

To Mormon leaders who abuse homosexuals: Your sin is self righteousness in believing you have any authority to act in the name of or in judgment for God; Your pretense of love for individuals you condemn based upon spurious belief systems which you have created and promulgated; Your belief in the efficacy of patriarchal control over the masses including women whom you have suppressed as second class members of society.

Your reward and punishment is deprivation of the concocted blessings of celestial polygamous marriage and hope of becoming gods as well as light, learning and understanding.

In times past, blinded by a spurious concept of Christianity, society has killed atheists, burned witches, marshaled armies against heathen and beaten and bullied persons it has subjected to slavery. Thanks to enlightenment, those sins have been eliminated. The day has arrived for sins against God protected rights of the homosexual community to end.

Nowhere in this article do I deny the existence of a higher power for it has been my lot in life to have experienced it. Nor do I suggest that laws ought not be in place to have some semblance of civil control over the exercise of sexual freedoms which I suggest are God-given.

Protection of the innocent against rape, statutory or otherwise is required. Regulation as to the issue of propriety and decency as to the exercise of those freedoms is appropriate.

No civil statutes ought to be enacted which restrict sexual affairs between consenting adults nor any discriminatory laws or practices against the equal civil rights of those persons. Without exception, persons of same sex wishing to have the status of marriage and all the ramifications that status brings should not be denied that right on account of sexual orientation.

If the state has not yet grown up in its recognition of that right and does not wish to extend the license (proactive) for such unions it should enact legislation (passive) which grants an acknowledgement of marital status (Common Law) of two same sex adults upon request by issuing a certificate of marriage without the fanfare of a license to marry. A ceremony of marriage is not the concern of the state or the church.

KNOW THIS THAT EVERY SOUL IS FREE
To choose his life and what he'll be;
For this eternal truth is given:
That God will force no man to heaven.
He'll call, persuade, direct aright,
And bless with wisdom, love, and light,
In nameless ways be good and kind,
But never force the human mind.
                    Anonymous 18th Century

35

ORGANIZED RELIGION: RACKETEERING INFLUENCED CORRUPT ORGANIZATIONS ALAMODE?

In the days of the Pharaohs, the Priests of the Egyptian God Horus used the timeless stratagem of the protection racket to allow the Pharaohs to keep the masses in a state of subservience to themselves as a God of the masses when in reality the Pharaohs were themselves in subservience to the god Horus by paying tribute to the priests who allowed the Pharaohs to so reckon themselves.

And of course the workers worked their asses off to please the non-producing Pharaohs who could in turn transfer a portion of the gross domestic product to the priests of Horus who in turn sat on their non productive asses while laughing all the way to the bank.

When the Israelites finally obtained their freedom from the Pharaohs, the old racket was re-invented much the same as the one the Pharaohs and the Egyptian masses continued to labor under. It was called a "tithe" which allegedly equated to ten percent of the possession or income of the masses. According to scripture, Moses was of the tribe of Levi, son of Jacob later named Israel. Aaron was Moses' brother and he and his tribe became the new priests of Hor. So the Levitical priests sat on their asses and collected a percentage of the gross domestic product of the masses of Israel which was or would be in addition to any tax for government.

When I say sat on their asses, I don't mean there was no effort to appear to be working for "god" with all kinds of trappings, "holiness" appearances and ceremony to justify the racket.

From these historical traditions we have the Christian syndrome of paying tribute to support a system of "holiness" and trappings of "godliness" enshrouded within the confines of some thousand or so entities all supported by the racket of religion.

There have been any number of racketeering parasites living off the masses who have been converted to indulge in the vagaries of this or that version of the concept of god and how to please that god and how to assure oneself of the earned gift of salvation from the darkened grave of eternal death and nothingness! Stupid man!

In modern times the scam continues. The former Rajneesh of Oregon, Elizabeth Prophet of Montana,

Thomas Monson of Utah, Pat Robertson of Washington, etcetera, etcetera, etcetera ad infinitum. All preaching absolutism without any empirical evidence other than the repetitious quotes of one racketeering con artist of that of another through the centuries all attempting to build a believable compilation of man uttered words and writings attributed to God. At least back to the unbelievable story of Adam and Eve according to Judaism, Christian(ism), and Islamism!

Excuse me there is at last one exception in that list and that is the scam of racketeer Joseph Smith of Book of Mormon fame and his today's alleged successor Thomas Monson of Utah.

Having been from birth a faithful heir to parentally seduced members of that brand of racketeering, I broke from it when Monson's predecessors failed to answer the ultimate question; prove your authority from God. They failed and Monson can do no better other than to rely upon spurious writings quoting his predecessors claims of authority. He has never had a vision and if he did he would be totally ashamed to speak in detail of it. Yet he is the esteemed, Prophet, Seer and Revelator of the Mormon Church.

Rather than going into the full spurious history of Mormonism, let's talk about the three basic elements of the racketeering package that it presents to delude and steal from its followers.

1. At the bottom of the list is that the Book of Mormon contains a promise the book will prove itself truthful by way of a prayerful asking of God if it is not true. If the searcher asks God with real intent having faith in God, the truth of the book will be made manifest by the Holy Ghost by a "burning in the bosom!"

If one reads it, then prays and does not get a "burning of the bosom" the fault is not in the untruth of the book but rather a failure of the searcher to meet the criteria needed for an affirmation.

2. The foundation of the church lies in it being the product of a restoration of actual priesthood of God upon the earth which Mormonism claims was lost from the earth after the apostolic era. This "priesthood" of God comes in two forms.

A. Aaronic Priesthood: This is the old Levitical priesthood by which money was extracted as tithe from Jews and their kindred. How was this obtained? By con artist Smith and seduced cohort Oliver Cowdrey while standing in the Susquehanna River in Pennsylvania and being ordained by the resurrected John the Baptist on May 15, 1929.

B. Melchizedek Priesthood: Supposedly this is a higher priesthood with real authority from God to do the more important things than simple ministering to the needs of people. It is required to bind on Earth and in heaven those things which only God can do but since he can't be everywhere at once he needs to have deputies to do it for him. How did Smith and Cowdrey obtain this priesthood? A month later <u>sometime</u> in June 1829 when Apostles Peter, James and John "appeared" to them as resurrected beings and ordained them by the laying on of hands!

Unfortunately these four resurrected beings were not able to write as they failed to execute any tangible certificates of ordination to the two racketeers by which they could produce evidence of their priesthood authority. A great leap of faith is required to accept this along with some real fast talking snake oil salesmanship known as brainwashing!

3. Having accepted the truth of the first two foundations of Mormonism i.e., Book of Mormon and priesthood, the ultimate exercise in racketeering is the selling of promises by the authority of the Melchizedek Priesthood, the right to have eternal sex in the hereafter with plural wives.

These promises are made in "Holy" Temples of God only to candidates who prove they have paid a full tribute to the church consisting of one tenth of income plus miscellaneous gifts of money for church and temple building funds along with once a month fast offerings and supporting missionaries in the field and unwavering subordination to the 15 top church leaders!

The selling of indulgences by the Catholic Church in times past for members to buy forgiveness from sin was a very cute act of racketeering but the Mormon racket of selling the right of eternal sex by far out does it!

Now to address the other sinister aspect of Mormon racketeering which I referred to in a recent article on Opednews.

This deals with the commission of crime by an arm of the church leadership which is surreptitiously engaged in the process of protecting the image of the church by any means justifiable to meet the end goal of Mormonism which is to take control of the earth as vice regents of Christ through the so-called millennium of peace.

Danites or avenging angels was an early established security/avenging organization of the church which surreptitiously honed obedience to early church leaders Joseph Smith, Jr. and Brigham Young while eliminating enemies. Most dictionaries have listed these marauders,

Orin Porter Rockwell is a well known non Mormon who served Smith and Young well into the Utah episode. "Backlotting" was his expertise to take care of dissidents.

The Springfield Murders to eliminate dissidents seeking to get out of the Utah territory to prevent unsavory reports of life in Mormon Utah Territory.

Using the Salt Lake police to embarrass Federal territorial judges and officers by hiring Prostitutes in San Francisco to work specially built houses with secret hallways where cops could peek through walls to spy on sexual activity for arrest and discredit of those officials all to keep Young in control of the territory.

The Mountain Meadows Massacre in the late 1850s is well documented. This was the execution of the blood atonement doctrine or justified murder.

The Morrisite war in Ogden Canyon to kill all men and boys opposed to Young.

The massacre of the Captain John Gunnison Survey Party, at Sevier Lake southwest of Delta, Utah occurred in October 1853 to keep the railroad from passing near Salt Lake City.

No I am not an atheist! But I know and understand that the special power that has created the universe (Cosmos) earth, man, animals, plants and life as we understand it does not walk about the "heavens" in a long trailing robe with a beard looking like the father of the popular image of Jesus!

Mankind's ego demands that God appear in the similitude of man, not of animal's insects or plants. Yet he who is attributed to finding God and writing Genesis (Moses) only answered to words uttered out of a burning bush. Therefore there is no affirmable image of God who may appear at will to any of us as anything anytime needed to convey a message.

We can only worship God by honoring God's creations, the earth and its mineral/gaseous composition, its inhabitants, both aquatic and mammals and the environment in which we as mammals have our being

36

Religion: Sacred cow of the U.S. Supreme Court

Jan 26, 2012

Nearly forty years ago I attempted to gain a comprehensive legal definition of religion. To my dismay, I discovered that there is no legal definition. Indeed religion can only be defined by what it is not! It seems as though the separation clause of the U.S. Constitution disallows the courts to define religion [or so they think] because it would somehow codify religion which is forbidden as an act of "respecting" it. The Constitution offers no such limitation on the court's overview of religion. Hence the court has taken on the role of supreme protector of religion without identifying what religion is.

My concern arose because of the unique position I was in as an attorney. I had recently broken the binds which had bound me close to my membership in the Mormon Church. It had taken over five years of struggle with church leaders.

Because of the international notoriety gained from that action, I received many requests from members of various denominations not only of the Mormon Church to come to their aid as against the, [what shall I say?] the "ungodly" action of their respective churches against them.

Foremost were the actions of the Mormon Church by way of its subordinate levels of priesthood administration who led the discrimination against those members who for some reason or other had taken an intellectual position antagonist to the published or preached ecclesiastical position or doctrines of the subordinate order. [The *church (Mormon Church per se) is the creation of the Melchizedek Priesthood. The priesthood came first and the church second in the order of "re-establishment". As such they are two separate but entwined entities with the priesthood superior to the church]*

In non-Mormon situations as well, the pleas I received were mostly about "shunning"; the practice of alienation of former members of any particular order which included breaking up families by practices of members and the hierarchy of those orders.

Clergy advising the one partner to divorce the other in order to save the woman or the man [depending on the offender] from being dragged into the kingdom of "Satan" and thus save them from a destiny of hell. Protecting the children of the union from a loss of faith thus preserving the membership well being of the order is always at issue.

Economic sanctions against the offender are another action of the order. From Utah I received complaints from many professionals who were driven out of business due to the overbearing presence of the church in the lifestyles of members. Medical doctors and dentists who lost patients; pharmacists who could not gain or keep employment within their community.

In one case I was advised that a prominent medical doctor had been excommunicated because he had looked of the corpse of John Singer, a notorious Mormon fundamentalist, who had been shot in the back with a 12 gauge shotgun blast. The viewing was in the mortuary and his client was the widow of victim Singer. The charge against the doctor was "cavorting with a known excommunicant". It was a sad thing to have to report to the doctor that there was nothing I could do about it.

And I heard from Utah farmers who had to compete against the church economically in the production and sale of agricultural products. The church operating out of tax free property and using donated labor in its production.

After all the legal reasoning as to why Churches do not have to comply with civil law as foisted on the legal community by the court, the final insult is the weak argument that as a member of a church, the individual feeling damaged has only the recourse of leaving the church. And of course uprooting completely because of shunning. The underlying argument is, **"you joined the church and so you are bound by its rules no matter how they may**

be offensive to the bill of rights of the U.S. Constitution".

That argument fails to recognize the fact that the majority of church members are born into and brainwashed in the order from infancy never having been able to exercise free will about the faith in the first place That brainwashing comes about by the scurrilous doctrine that the parents will be heavenly rewarded only if they raise their children in the faith.

I argue how any organization deals with its members has to be protected by the Bill of rights or any other law made out of the Bill of Rights which deal with employment issues in which members or non members of a social order religious or otherwise are affected. Employment being a physical non religious matter easily determined non-religious in nature.

To give free reign to religion to deal with its members or society in general in any manner that can easily be determined non-religious in nature is totally wrong. It does in fact allow for the creation of racketeering influenced corrupt organizations [RICO] seeking shelter from prosecution. In my observation, the vast majority of religious organizations are clearly a racket against God and humanity.

Yes it is true, that the founding fathers wished to see no state sponsored religion adopted by government. But the founding fathers did not intend that rules of equity would be abandoned by the courts in favor of organized religion. Equity was the child of the Church of England and it was designed to give relief to church members who were being wronged by the church. These wrongs were righted by the courts of Chancery. While we do have equity in our laws it unwittingly stops at the door of the church.

As with corporate privileges beginning with **Santa Clara County v. Southern Pacific Railroad Company**, 118 U.S. 394 (1886) and recently **Citizens United v. Federal Election Commission**, 558 U.S. 08-205 (2010) , 558 U.S. , 130 S. Ct. 876 (January 21, 2010, Ruling corporations as "persons", The Supreme Court has also read into the separation clause conditions which the founders never intended.

(The) "Congress shall make no law respecting an establishment of religion or prohibiting the full exercise thereof;"" [U.S. **Constitution; Amendment I]** does not grant to the courts the right to allow religion to harm anyone in any way, member or not.

The two words which come into play are "respect-ing" and "regard-ing"

Respect or respecting means: admiration, esteem, consideration, appreciation, deference, reverence, veneration, courtesy, politeness, civility, attentiveness, etc.

"Regard" can have similar definitions but if it were properly used in the Separation clause it would mean "in reference to".

"The Congress shall not make any law (in reference to) religion nor any law prohibiting the free exercise thereof."

What has happened is that the Congress has made laws respecting (favoring) religion and that has been supported by the Supreme Court with the pretense that it has not.

Among the laws respecting religion, the Congress has by way of the tax code given respect to religion by favoring its exercise by church members allowing them to deduct the tithes and donations paid to it from personal income taxes as well as incomes to the church from any source it receives them. The result is a non reportable amassing of wealth by religion. Another result is imposing a larger tax burden on non-religious citizens to cover the expenses of government not supported by religion or its tithe paying members.

The argument used in defense of such unconstitutional action is that the church as a charity is providing for assistance to masses saving the government from the cost of such services. Problem here is that the government has no duty to provide the ministrations of religion in the first place!

The recent resolution of the congress that the expression of "In God we trust" is a part of the constitutional but unspoken order of governmental intent of the founding fathers is a gross violation of the separation Clause.

What we really have is a fear by the members of the Congress and the courts that they themselves may be in line of fire of God if they should in anyway offend God. To follow the Constitution those individuals are required to act independent of their own religious philosophy and fears in delivering laws [and interpretations] pure and absent any **respect** for religion or religion's questionable quest.

The observations of Founders like George Washington who never saw the hand of God in the known history of the world despite all of the prayers of all the masses of humanity, clergy and lay alike ought to be considered by all of us.

Who among us can prove that God has answered our prayers? We can assert He/She has but we cannot prove it.

Indeed in my own life I was troubled by the long forgotten details of what is termed an epiphany these days when I was struck by a light on my eighth birthday. It took me thirty nine years to obtain a recall. When I did finally obtain that recall it was only after I had followed promptings to ordain a young Black male to Mormon priesthood. I had exhausted five years seeking the answer to that dilemma by beseeching top church leaders only to find they were impotent to give me an answer simply because they were not only impotent but imposters to what I had been taught they were all my life.

And so **I know*** , but I cannot prove outside my own experiences [began on May 8, 1937 culminating of June 9, 1978] that God has great foreboding over the quest for empire of the Mormon Church, presently personified by the Presidential candidacy of W. Mitt Romney. [Wasn't it strange that two Mormons, Romney and Huntsman were seeking the office when church membership is only around two percent of US population?]

I write, I speak but my message falls on deaf ears. Ears deafened by time and the forgotten history of the United States verses the Mormon problem. That problem was well known by presidents between the time of 1844 and 1906. That problem was one of the establishment of a kingdom within the United States converting democracy to theocracy headed by the president of the Mormon Church. **See Mormon Doctrine: Bruce McConkie: 1966 pages 415-417.**

We are on the threshold of a critical examination of that issue this year 2012. As a nation we have forgotten our history but the Mormon Church has not lost sight of its goal which it has suspended since obtaining statehood of Utah in the late nineteenth century.

As an attorney, I am crippled from bringing these issues into a court of law simply because the court would base its opinion on the years of unjustified rulings by the U.S. Supreme Court ruling the matter to be First Amendment non-judicial thus granting a safe harbor for religion [Mormon Church] to defeat the Constitution of the United States allowing it to establish its "Kingdom of God on Earth" with the Mormon President as "earth King".

However, if I had the support of people of the United States who would fund the cause I would yet again file a lawsuit to keep Mr. Romney from seeking the presidency and staking an eternal objection against any faithful Mormon from seeking that presidency ad infinitum! In the process, Americans would begin to understand the seriousness of the problem of religion interfering with a free government. Or of government respecting it!

Is there anyone out there who wishes to set up a legal fund to accomplish this? It is far more important than funding any candidate for the office of president!

This article does not address the 1878 issue of Supreme Court interference with polygamy as a religious doctrine taught Mormons and off-shoot fundamentalists who continue to follow the 132nd Section of the unchanged wording of the Doctrine and Covenants of the Mormon Church. That issue will need to be resolved at a later time. See **Reynolds v. United States,** 98 U.S. 145 (1878)

NEXT SECTION OF

LETTERS SENT TO RESPONSIBLE GOVERNMENTAL PERSONS WITH NO RESPONSE COMING FROM THEM AS PER THE "TYRANNY OF SILENCE"NOTICED BY MANY CRITICS OF THE MORMON CHURCH WHO LABELED THE CHURCH HIERARCHY

"THE MARBLE PALACE MOB" IN REFERENCE TO CHURCH HEADQUARTERS AT 47 EAST SOUTH TEMPLE SALT LAKE CITY, UTAH.

It appears that even the president of the United States and all his cabinet are presently acting as stooges to the Mormon Hierarchy

AMERICANS UNITED AGAINST FASCIST & THEOCRATIC GOVERNMENT

INCORPORATION AS A NONPROFIT pending
TEMPORARY ADDRESS   PO BOX 60958   RENO, NEVADA 89506

George Washington's Birthday
February 22, 2011

President Barack Obama
White House
1600 Pennsylvania Ave.
Washington D.C.

National Security Agency
Fort George Meade, Maryland 20755-6000

Eric Holder Attorney General
U.S. Department of Justice
950 Pennsylvania Avenue, NW
Washington, DC 20530-0001

Secretary Janet Napolitano
U.S. Department of Homeland Security
Washington, DC 20528

RE: CONSTRUCTION OF NSA UTAH DATA CENTER

President Obama, Gentlemen and Madam:

I am writing this letter to express my concern about the construction of the NSA Data Center in the State of Utah as reported by NSA Press Release, 6 January 2011.

This concern is based on the historical fact that the primary political force in the state of Utah is the Church of Jesus Christ of Latter-day Saints. It is no secret and indeed an historical fact that the Church leadership is and has always been hostile to the extended interests of the Republic of the United States overtly or covertly.

President Obama
White House
National Security Agency
Eric Holder Attorney General
U.S Justice Department
Secretary Janet Napolitano
U.S. Department of Homeland Security

February 22, 2011
Page 2.

If you research the history of the church, its claimed persecutions by the government of the United States, together with the candidacy for president of the United States of church founder Smith, building the data center in Utah is playing into the hands and long term planning of the church entity in its ultimate goal of establishing itself as the sole theocratic world government. It would be interesting to discover who lobbied for the building in Utah! Sen. Orin Hatch? Former Sen. Robert Bennett? Sen. Harry Reid? Sen. Mike Crapo? Rep. Rob Bishop? Rep. Jason Chaffetz? Rep. Jake Flake? Rep. Dean Heller? Rep. Wally Herger? Rep. Jim Matheson? Rep. Buck McKeon? Rep. Mike Simpson? Rep. Eni Faleomavaega? The Heritage Foundation? Other Mormons?

In the early 1960's the church began its own electronic surveillance of potential political enemies by the use of a system created under the direction of Mormon Bill Gay (now deceased) of Summa Corporation Fame. The use of a golden Bee shaped lapel pin worn by agents of the church was a Microwave cavity resonator used to covertly assemble intelligence for dossiers to be stored by the church in a secret location. The design was patterned after the Soviet electronic intrusion into the US Embassy in Moscow. He (Gay) and the group called the Mormon Mafia had control of the assets and the person of Howard Hughes between the Late 1950's and 1971 when he (Hughes) was "kidnapped" out of the Desert Inn Casino in Las Vegas. Then taken down the rear fire escape. A group of ex-CIA, FBI and Military intelligence personnel were organized to conduct the operation. Indeed it is likely that each of you have your own dossier in the Mormon vault.

It was news to the world on the 5th day of April 1976 that the body of Hughes had been taken from Acapulco, MX to Houston Texas and buried in an unmarked grave.

You will remember the infamous Mormon Will of Hughes which was delivered to the Las Vegas probate Court by Mormon Church legal Counsel Wilford Kirton and later discredited.

There is plausible suspicion that the body interred in Texas was not that of Hughes but a double and that his remains are in a location under the control of the Mormon Church in the state of Utah. When Brigham Young led the Saints out of Illinois in 1846 toward what later became the Utah territory, his intention was to begin the establishment of the Mormon earthly kingdom which was to ultimately control the world as the Kingdom of God on Earth. Yet later, the actions of President Polk to order the US army to invade Mexico causing a "Border conflict" resulting in the treaty of Guadalupe Hidalgo 1848 which conveyed the territory of six western states to the US fulfilling the manifest destiny of certain nut cases beginning with the pilgrims. We are all aware Abraham Lincoln as member of the House of Representatives criticized Polk for that illegal action

No Mormon for President

President Barack Obama
National Security Agency
Eric Holder Attorney General
U.S Justice Department
Secretary Janet Napolitano
U.S. Department of Homeland Security

February 15, 2011
Page 3

Brigham Young was the governor "king" of Deseret, His name for his "Kingdom" and late territorial governor of Utah for a time during which the Alexander Fancher wagon train in route to California was massacred in September 1857 by Mormons clad as Indians. The Saints were stirred up to a war fever against the United States by the rhetoric of Young. Outnumbered by Johnston's army Young then suspended his plan for the Kingdom of God. **Let me repeat SUSPENDED!**

When, by actions of the Congress, the Mormons were forced to cede the practice of polygamy, the ceding was by manifesto of Wiford Woodruff and not by revelation from God. After escheating the property of the church by the Federal government, the practice was suspended to regain the wealth of the church. Let **me repeat SUSPENDED** although the practice does continue among renegades who follow the teachings of church founder Smith as a duty to God and in secret by top church officials. The pertinent teaching of polygamy is section 132 of the Doctrine and Covenants of the church which is recorded as a revelation of God, has not been vacated or repealed. That practice is believed to be a divinely given commandment called the "New and everlasting Covenant". Most Mormon women today have no understanding of the suspended nature of the "revelation".

But back to the issue of intelligence gathering by the LDS church for the past 50 years. I worked in the church building Department in the church headquarters as a young returned missionary with a history of construction experience having been the Mission Architect of the then British Mission. This was in the early 1950's. My immediate superior was Julian Cannon. Some twenty years late in September, 1972 Julian had finally been named as the chairman of the Church Building Department [All prior chairman were cronies of church leaders.] I met with him and his associate Paul Woodruff both of whom were being forced into retirement since they had reached the age of 65 with no social security or retirement compensation from the church after working there for their entire lives right out of the University of Utah. However, Julian was given a reprieve until the church office tower had been completed as that was his project.

At that meeting I learned that the very top [4] floors of the building were to be incomplete when he was forced to retire so that some else would supervise the completion. I asked him why and he responded, **"Beats the hell out of me but it is built like a fortress!"** That statement confirmed the learning some five years earlier that I had received that the surveillance system built by Summa Corp under Bill Gay would be suspended until the church tower had been completed as it needed space to store the files [Dossiers] of suspect persons whom the church could move against when they attempted to "save the Constitution".

It has been stated that Patience is a virtue. The LDS church is very patient in waiting for the opportunity to "take and posses" the government of the United States but that act is not a virtue!

268

President Barack Obama
National Security Agency
Eric Holder Attorney General
U.S Justice Department
Secretary Janet Napolitano
U.S. Department of Homeland Security

February 22, 2011
Page 4

The U.S. government, in building its intelligence storage facility in the area of covert control of the Mormon Church is a very frightening thought to those of us as former Mormons who are aware of the conspiracy to "take and posses the government" under pretense of "saving the Constitution" The massive files not only of the United States but the world at large stored there will, you can be assured, be under the ultimate control of the Mormon "Prophet" President, Presently Thomas Monson, to whom all priesthood holders have taken a secretly sworn temple ceremonious blood oath, of total subservience. That includes Mitt Romney and all of the Mormon members of the Congress I have listed!

Should former Massachusetts Governor Mitt Romney* be elected president and commander in chief of the armed forces in 2012 all the forces necessary would be in place for the coup! It would destroy the Republic and turn it into a theocracy not unlike Islam and its Sharia law!

I am requesting that you immediately halt all construction work on the data center project to allow time to fully investigate the charges I am making. If you fail to do so I will organize a public effort to seek an injunction against further construction at the site regardless of its stage of progress!

Yours truly,
Americans United Against Fascist & Theocratic Government

/S/_____
Douglas A. Wallace, Esq.
Director pro tem

* You have to understand that it is not an issue of church affiliation or of a litmus test prohibited by the Constitution but rather the Holy Temple sworn blood oath of Romney, et al to be subservient to the Mormon President and his Counselors in all things, which includes the Mormon quest for empire.
See: http://www.opednews.com/populum/manage.php?submit=view&storyid=47902

REFERENCES:
Millennial Messenger March-April 1978 Available at University of Utah Marriott Library
Charles Wood, The Mormon Conspiracy;   Doug Wallace, Under the Mormon Tree,
Klaus J. Hansen, Quest for Empire, The Political Kingdom of God and the Council of Fifty in Mormon History,
Hyrum L. Andrus, Joseph Smith and World Government
Bruce McKonkie, Mormon Doctrine, Kingdom of God pps 415-417

No Mormon for President

Americans United Against Fascist and Theocratic Government

PO Box 60958 Reno, NV 89506

May 24, 2011

60 Minutes
524 West 57th St.
New York, NY 10019

RE: Construction of NSA Intelligence Storage Facility in Utah

To All Reporters:

After watching the segment of 60 minutes concerning Thomas Drake I am persuaded to submit the attached materials which concerns a gross mismanagement of funding by NSA in the locating of the massive storage facility in Utah.

Time is a forgiving element in the course of history but it is certain to force a repeat of history to the possible demise of democracy as we have known it by the ignorant committing of a Coup D'etet against democracy by NSA and certain moles within the Congress.

Sincerely,

Douglas A. Wallace

Attachments: 1- Letter to House and Senate Armed Services committees May 24, 2011

2. Letter to Inspector General DOD, May 24, 2011

3. Letter to Obama, et al in re construction of storage facility February 22, 2011

Email addresses: director@americans-united-against-fascist-and-theocratic-government.org

octogenarious@gmail.com

Americans United Against Fascist and Theocratic Government

PO Box 60958 Reno, NV 89506

May 24, 2011

United States Senate Armed Services Committee
Room SR-228, Russell Senate Office Building
Washington, DC 20510-6050

United States House of Representatives Armed Services Committee

2120 Rayburn House Office Bldg.
Washington, DC 20515

To all Members of both Committees: Please distribute

RE: Construction of NSA Intelligence Storage Facility in Utah

The attached letter to the DOD Office of Inspector General together with the attached materials is self explanatory.

It is time for both committees to take action to prevent the Mormon Quest for Empire agenda from becoming a reality. A nation that forgets its history is likely doomed to repeat it. Research the Utah Wa of 1857 and all that it implied as a part of your investigation.

Yours truly,

Douglas A. Wallace, JD.

director@americans-united-against-fascist-and-theocratic-governmnet.org

octogenarious@gmail.com

Attachments

SEE LETTER TO DEPARTMENT OF DEFENSE INVESTIGATOR GENERAL

BELOW:

Americans United Against Fascist and Theocratic Government

PO Box 60958 Reno, NV 89506

May 24, 2011

Department of Defense Office of Inspector General
400 Army Navy Drive
Arlington, VA 22202-4704

RE: Construction of NSA intelligence Storage Facility in Utah

Gentlemen,

I stand opposed to the construction of the above referenced facility in the state of Utah. I attach hereto a copy of a letter directed to the White House, Homeland Security, the Justice Department and the Arm Corp of Engineers. I have not received a reply from any of the addressees.

The reasons for the opposition have been well stated in the referenced letter as well as are laid out by the contents of the website: www.americans-against-fascist-and-theocratioc-government.org

As a former member of the LDS [Mormon] Church I am painfully aware of the secret ambition of the church to become the physical and political government of the world. This agenda is disguised by the overt patriotism espoused by both the leaders and the priesthood of that church.

While the members of the Church may well believe that they are sincere in that patriotism, the leaders are being less than honest. In my book, *Under the Mormon Tree*, www.underthemormontree.com , I have exposed the past 40 year covert intelligence gathering activities of the church spying on American and peoples of other nations to achieve their ultimate goal. Building the storage facility in Utah is givin; the fox the job of guarding the hen house. DOD has unwittingly committed a coup d'état supported by Mormon Moles in the Congress.

Please investigate these concerns. As a retired attorney I have contemplated taking legal action seeking an injunction. However I will defer doing that for a reasonable time to allow you to make an investigation of these issues. I do not address the issue of warrantless spying on Americans by NSA but am cognizant of that activity.

The church has covertly done that for years. I will be available for consultation if the need may arise. M email addresses are below.

Yours truly,

/s/Douglas A. Wallace, JD.

director@americans-united-against-fascist-and-theocratic-government.org

octogenarious@gmail.com   Enclosures:

Mormon Dissident Requests Church President Thomas S. Monson to ask Romney and Huntsman to Withdraw from Presidential Race

May 14, 2012
By wp#admin

In a letter to Mormon President Thomas S. Monson, dated December 27, 2011, Douglas A. Wallace a dissident who brought about the racial equality of Black male Members of the church between 1976 and 1978 suggests that Monson take immediate action to:

1. Acknowledge and repudiate in public, the active concept and quest for a "Kingdom of God on Earth" to allegedly fulfill scripture with the church as political world kingship.

2. Requests that Monson require Mormon Presidential hopefuls Mitt Romney and Jon Huntsman, to withdraw from 2012 Presidential race by January 5, 2012.

If these demands are not timely met Wallace believes the Mormon Church will suffer an embarrassing impact. In his letter to the Mormon President he maintains that the Mormon Church's goal of trying to establish a "Kingdom of God on earth" is contrary to Providential will. He also mentions that God will destroy the need of Mormon temples by setting Mormon followers free from the "bondage of the Church."

In his letter Wallace alludes to his past confrontation with Mormon Church authorities when he ordained the black priest 1976. He did this to fulfill his belief in equality of race. This led to Wallace being excommunicated by the Mormon Church.

he states that he gave the church leaders two months to meet with him before January 1, 1976. He stated that if they didn't he would consider himself insubordinate and follow dictates of conscience. When they failed to meet with him he gave notice of that insubordination not knowing what the spirit would guide him to do.

The authorities then tried to spy on him using Russian KGB Micro-wave cavity resonation devices designed into lapel pins shaped as honey bees and worn by Home Teachers. Being aware of that system he avoided disclosure of his plans. In the end the church was taken by surprise on April 2, 1976 when Wallace ordained the black man. After two years the church relented and granted black male members to be ordained. Wallace called that his first mission.

The second or current mission is to expose and set aside Mormon Church ambitions to become the political head of world government. All church President Monson has to do is to comply with spiritual promptings given Wallace and dismantle the 1844 plan of world conquest. Actually Wallace is indifferent as to what action Monson will take. He has simply notified Monson of risks and what he does will determine the future of the church.

DEFINING "APOCALYPSE" BY TRUTHOUT
April 16, 2012

There are those who want us to believe that the end is nigh: That this coming together can't stop humanity's march to destruction, or that changing the status quo is itself "the apocalypse."

Apocalypse comes from the Greek word *apokálypsis*, meaning the "lifting of the veil," or "the disclosure of something hidden from the majority of mankind in an era dominated by falsehood and misconception."

The word apocalypse triggers deep feelings and intense reactions, because it has been used for so long as a mechanism of control: the ultimate threat, or the great reckoning in which divine forces pass judgment on humanity.

Instead of divine intervention accompanied by rivers of blood and fire, perhaps this idea of "lifting of the veil" is better understood as the revelation of a fundamental choice: do we, as a species, embrace our potential for good by realigning our intentions and our actions to come together in solidarity, solve our problems and work to reverse the damage we've done to the planet? Or do we choose the path of exploitation, separation and destruction?

Making this choice clear is the duty of the storytellers - the independent journalists and writers who use their time to try and make this choice clear.

Truthout e-news April 16, 2012

[messenger@truthout.org]

The 2012 Presidential election process and all its ramifications could well be the Apocalypse or the lifting of the Veil!

Author

SUMMARY

This book is not intended to humiliate or to offend members of the Mormon Faith yet there will be many who will be offended by it. The author has many relatives who are still faithful church members and he has made no effort to change their belief system.

Yet if they came to him with questions he would patiently explain his present position and how he got there.

That of course is explained in his memoirs, *Under the Mormon Tree*, Published two years ago. To date that has not happened. Nor does he expect it to happen as he knows how extremely difficult it is to confront the issue of having spent many years of one's life immersed in a faith that ultimately has no provable foundation beyond fiction and myth.

But the author makes no apology for expressions he has made after leaving the Mormon faith and seeing it as a threat to the world. That view is also held by the God of the universe as recorded by the author's 8th birthday event.

The purpose of the book then is to raise the flag of a clear and present danger to the non-Mormon populace that extreme caution needs to be taken when going to the polls this coming November and voting for a president of the United States. Assuming that Mitt Romney is nominated by the Republican National Convention as its candidate, alarm bells need to be set ringing. This work is intended to help that awareness.

It is also intended to point out a weakness in the Constitution regarding the First Amendment Separation clause as well as Religious Test clause of

Article 6 that needs to be addressed so that this kind of problem will not again be present in future election processes. Also visit:

www.americans-united-against-fascist-and-theocratic-government.org

also: www.underthemormontree.com

APPENDIX ONE

The following is a compressed copy of a lawsuit filed by the author on March 28, 2012 as an effort to put his finger in the dike to prevent the catastrophy of the fulfillment of the Mormon quest for empire. He makes no apology for the effort, recognizing that it is a long shot without a great deal of hope as is the nature of the crawling speed of lawsuits and the obsticles that will be placed in its path unless the American people awake and arise to prevent the Mormon Quest for Empire from happening it will happen inspite of these feeble efforts.

The United states District Courts are unlike state courts in that no lawsuit can be filed in the court that is not based upon items of legislation [statutes] of the Congress, the Constitution and Treaties

In addition, "Standing" to Sue is a definite requsite for any plaintiff seeking relief. The requirments of standing are:

1. Is there an injury of the plaintiff or a clear and present danger of injury.

2. Does the court have jurisdiction of the subject matter.

3. Can the court provide relief.

In this case the plaintiff is attempting to establish the three requirements of standing are met. He is using the case as a class action in which clear and present danger to the class is valid and that he as a retired attorney who has taken the oath prescribed by Article six, clause 3 of the US Constitution requiring that he swears to defend the Constitution against enemies domestic or foreign has given him standing

He has no illusions about the success of the effort as he knows that millions of Dollars would have to be raised to employ skilled legal counsel to assist in prosecuting the case.

He also knows that in the absence of legislation, i.e. a Constitutional amendment, many years of litigation will be needed to correct the course. Since we don't have that time it is important for Americans to wake up now!

Update...June 29, 2012. The complaint will be amended to better address the problems contained in the single sentence paragraph three of Article six. The complaint below reflects that as clause 3-A and Clause 3-B.

No Mormon for President

--------0-------

IN THE U.S. DISTRICT COURT FOR THE DISTRICT OF NEVADA AT RENO

Plaintiff in pro per
P.O. Box 60958, Reno NV 89506
Voice Mail 775-352-3824
Email: octogenarious@gmail.com

DOUGLAS A. WALLACE IN PRO PER for himself and
All persons similarly situated

_____/

Plaintiff(s)   FILED
                                                                   MAR 28

2012
vs.   Clerk US
District

                                                                   Court

WILLARD MITT ROMNEY, candidate for President   District of
Nevada
and ERIC HOLDER, Attorney General of the United
States and LYNNE M. HALBROOKS   3:12-cv-00167-
LRH-VPC
Acting Inspector General of the   [Stamp Facsimile]
Department of Defense

_____/

Defendants.

COMPLAINT FOR JUDICIAL RELIEF INJUNCTION AND MANDAMUS

NOW COMES Plaintiff, Douglas A. Wallace herein-after referred to as Plaintiff in pro per and as initial representative for the class of persons damaged by the allegations within this complaint. Plaintiff acknowledges that he is not a licensed attorney in the District and that Nevada counsel will have to be appointed to represent the class upon certification at least in Nevada and perhaps nationally. Plaintiff alleges as follows:

JURISDICTION AND VENUE

1. Plaintiff brings this action under Article VI, clause **3A** of the United States Constitution as a judicial officer sworn and bound to support and defend the Constitution against all enemies both domestic and foreign.

2. This Court has jurisdiction pursuant to 28 U.S. § 1331, which gives district courts original jurisdiction over civil actions arising under the Constitution, laws or treaties of the United States.

3. Venue is appropriate in this judicial district under 28 U.S.C. § 1391(b) because the events giving rise to this complaint affect this district as well as the nation as a whole.

PARTIES

4. Plaintiff is a citizen of the United States and resides in Washoe County, Nevada which is in this district. Plaintiff is also a member of the Bar of the State of Washington # 3733 but not in active practice as he elected in 2002 to be placed on the non-disciplinary suspended list for personal reasons. As such, while he is suspended from the practice of law in the state of Washington in both State and Federal District Courts he is still an officer of the State and Federal court system and is also admitted to the Tenth Circuit. His allegations of potential injury include himself and all Americans.

5. Defendant WILLARD MITT ROMNEY, herein after referred to as ROMNEY is a candidate for the national office of President of the

United States and maintains campaign offices in the district. He is a High Priest holder of the Melchizedek Priesthood which is the parent organization of the Church of Jesus Christ of Latter-day Saints more commonly referred to as Mormon or LDS Church.

The unique status of ROMNEY is that he has taken solemn oaths in LDS temples to dedicate and consecrate in his life and property to the total subservience of the top leaders of that church which it will be shown have had a 168 year agenda of securing the presidency of the United States in order to establish a theocracy which constitutes their concept of Zion and the kingdom of God on earth. ROMNEY, like nearly every male priesthood holder of the said church has been brainwashed to believe that the day will come when the priesthood of that the church will take over the government of the United States in order to "save" the constitution. As such he is the perfect Manchurian Candidate.

6. Defendant ERIC HOLDER herein after referred to as HOLDER is the Attorney General of the United States and maintains offices in this district through the office of United States Attorney. His responsibility is to defend the government of the United States and its citizens from the
criminal and conspiratorial actions of individuals and corporations.

7. Defendant LYNNE M. HALBROOKS hereinafter referred to as HALBROOKS, is the acting Inspector General of the United States Department of Defense responsible for making sure that all actions of the Department of Defense are conducted according to civil and military law
and the U.S. Constitution. Her supervisory responsibility extends over the National Security Agency [NSA] which is the electronic spying agency of the Department of Defense.

GENERAL ALLEGATIONS

8. Amendment I of the United States Constitution forbids the Congress from making any law respecting an establishment of religion. Under Supreme Court rulings, District courts have voluntarily adopted a policy of non interference in the affairs of religion. Additionally, Article VI, clause 3 B of the Constitution forbids a religious (litmus) test to be applied as a Qualification to any office or public trust under the United States.

9. The courts have not defined religion simply because any attempt to do so will infringe upon the self imposed prohibition of making laws or rules regarding religion. The only way that religion can be defined is in what acts, actions or posture it does are not definable as "religion". That is, what religion is, may not be defined as such by what common sense would tell us it is not.

10. As a result of that judicial policy, a chasm, an abyss if you will, has been inadvertently created by the courts between what it might or might not consider to be "religion" to which a litmus test may or may not be constitutionally applied.

11. Within that chasm [abyss], religion has made bold entrance with impunity to inflict upon its own members, rules creating personal injury and damage that would not be allowed in a clearly non-religious situation.

12. Sedition can be defined as communication or agreement which has as its objective the overthrow or reformation of the existing forms of government of any nation or state. Also,

publications or speeches tending to disturb the tranquility of the state or an insurrectionary
movement tending towards treason but wanting an overt act is sedition.

13. When sedition is an ever present element within any particular "religious" organization, the question has to arise in a legal sense under the United States Constitution or interpretations of it in any U.S. court. Therefore the question present in this complaint is this: Is sedition to be defined as a protected religious activity as applied to Constitution Article VI, clause 3 and thus non-justiciable by the courts, or is it to be a non-privileged act susceptible to the scrutiny of the court. If the latter, then the court must take upon itself a scrutiny of that part of "religion" in order to protect the rights of citizens against the harm or damage that a
successful seditious agenda of any particular "religious" entity would impose. In doing this the court must take liberty to examine which aspects of the "religion" are clearly non-protected. That scrutiny must be applied before the sedition is an accomplished fact. Plaintiff is asking the court to now indulge in that review.

14, Defendant ROMNEY as afore stated is a committed member of a religious organization historically recognized as a seditious organization which will be shown in detail hereafter. Plaintiff asserts the court has a duty to separate the "wheat" from the "chaff" and determine that the seditious portion of that organization to which ROMNEY is committed is a justiciable portion as non protected by the religious litmus test of Article VI, clause 3.

15 Defendant HOLDER is the primary public legal official sworn to oath to protect and defend the Constitution against all enemies

both foreign and domestic. Plaintiff asserts that the action he is taking in filing this complaint is properly the obligation and duty of HOLDER and that due

diligence is HOLDER'S responsibility not that of the plaintiff or of the class to be protected herein. The plaintiff will show hereafter that defendant HOLDER has been asked to investigate allegations made in this complaint* but that he has refused to so act. Plaintiff asserts that the

court should issue a writ of Mandamus to Holder mandating that he investigate the allegations of this complaint and bring to justice any and all individuals responsible for what is clearly a conspiracy accomplished to allow the surfacing of a 168 year old plan for the LDS Church to take and "possess the government of the United States and then through it, the world. * SEE EXHIBIT 1

16. Defendant HALBROOKS is the duly appointed individual to make certain that the U.S. Department of defense acts within the scope of its franchise enumerated by the applicable laws and constitutional constraints. Plaintiff asserts that the National Security Agency [NSA] is a part of that responsibility, Plaintiff asserts and alleges that she, as acting Inspector General has failed to act in the best interests of the United States Constitution in allowing the continued construction of a NSA data storage facility in the state of Utah where it can and will be used to

support, sustain and enable the seditious actions of a Coup'd'état of the religious but seditious organization that defendant ROMNEY is committed to serve. Plaintiff asserts he has notified Defendant HALBROOKS or her predecessor*, the former Inspector General of DOD which makes her privy to the notice, of dangers but the defendant has refused to act in the best interests of plaintiff(s) or of the U.S. Constitution. Plaintiff asserts that the court should issue a writ of Mandamus to defendant HALBROOKS mandating that she suspend construction of the UTAH DATA CENTER and investigate the allegations of seditious conduct of the

LDS Church and its quest for Empire before resuming construction. * SEE EXHIBIT 2 ATTACHED.

17. While the seditiously liable religious organization known informally as the LDS Church is not named as a defendant herein, its impact upon the committed life and loyalty of defendant ROMNEY needs to be examined and addressed as a part of the justiciable non- religious aspect of the underlying motivation in bringing this lawsuit.

18. In 1976, U.S. Senator FRANK CHURCH of Idaho was given chair-manship of a committee to investigate the FISA abuses of domestic intelligence gathering by the NSA. Speaking of the potential dangers of over reach by NSA, he made the following statement as a result of that investigation:

19. *"That capacity **at any time** could be turned around on **the American people** and **no American would have any privacy left**; such [is] the capability to monitor everything: telephone conversations, telegrams, it doesn't matter. There would be no place to hide. **If government ever became a tyranny, if a Dictator ever took charge in this country**, the technological capacity of that the intelligence community has given the government could enable it to impose **total tyranny**, and there would be no way to fight back, because the most careful effort to combine together in resistance to the government, **no matter how privately it was done, is within the reach of the government to know**. Such is the capability of this technology"*. Emphasis added

NBC, Meet the Press August 17, 1975; The Shadow Factory, James Bamford; page 344

20. That statement was made 37 years ago and the technological advancement has quadrupled since that time. SEE EXHIIBT FOUR ATTACHED. Additionally, Frank Church is widely quoted in regards to the National Security Agency:

21. "I don't want to see this country ever go across the bridge... I know the capacity that is there to make tyranny total in America, and we must see to it that this Agency and all agencies that possess this technology operate within the law and under proper supervision, so that we never cross over that abyss. **That is the abyss from which there is no return."** The Shadow Factory, James Bamford

22. That abyss of which Church speaks could be equated with Caesar's crossing of the Rubicon which destroyed parliamentary democracy in the Roman Empire or of the Bolshevik Revolution of Lenin

23. Plaintiff asserts and alleges that the seditiuosly liable "religious" organization to which defendant Romney is committed by blood oath sworn obedience to blindly follow his priesthood superiors demands, has been about the business of spying on Americans and others since the
early 1970's. The accomplishment of securing the NSA facility in Utah will greatly assist it in achieving its goal of becoming the "Kingdom of God empire on planet earth" it will be the dictator feared by Senator Church in the above quotation.

24. Plaintiff alleges and asserts that evidence of the seditious intentions of the Religious entity of which ROMNEY is a member has been deliberately suppressed. That entity has, since the 2008 presidential elections, removed a certain book from the shelves of its owned Deseret Book Stores and caused a discontinuance of its printing. That book titled **Mormon Doctrine ***** written by a

high official of the entity, Bruce McConkie, clearly states the seditious intentions of that entity. From the book, the following is quoted: *** SEE EXHIBIT THREE ATTACHED

25. **Kingdom of God:** "The Church of Jesus Christ of Latter-day Saints **(Mormon or LDS)** as it is now constituted is the kingdom of God on earth; nothing more needs to be done to establish the kingdom. The Church and kingdom are one and the same." Pg 415 (Emphasis added)

26. "The Church or kingdom is not a democracy; legislation is not enacted by the body of people comprising the organization; they do not make the laws governing themselves. The Church is a kingdom, The Lord Jesus Christ is the Eternal King and the President of the Church, the mouthpiece of God on earth, is the earthly king. All things come to the Church from the King of the kingdom in heaven through the king of the kingdom on earth".
pg 416

27. "There is of course, the democratic principle of common consent where-under the people may accept or reject what the Lord offers to them. Acceptance brings salvation; rejection leads to damnation."
Pg 416

28. "During the millennium, the kingdom of God will continue on earth, but in that day it will be both an ecclesiastical and a political kingdom. That is the Church (which is the kingdom) will have the rule and government of the world given to it. When inspired teachers speak of the future setting up of the kingdom of God on earth, they have reference to the millennial day when the "The kingdoms of this world are become the kingdoms of our Lord and his Christ; and he shall reign forever and forever."(Rev. 11:15)

29. "Daniel also saw the day when *"the saints of the most High (LDS, I added)* shall *take and posses the kingdom forever and ever."* (Dan 7:18, 22, 27.) The Prophet (Joseph Smith) prayed that the present ecclesiastical kingdom of God on earth might roll forth that the future political and kingdom of God on earth might come". (Doctrine and Covenants (D&C) 65; Doctrines of Salvation, Vol. 1 pp 229-246.) pg 416

30. Defendant ROMNEY invested, as did this plaintiff, two years on a foreign mission for the Mormon Church ignorantly espousing sedition to citizens of those foreign nations under the code name of "Building up the Kingdom". ROMNEY believes in the position of the church with reference to its quest for empire as did the plaintiff prior to his awakening. If elected to the office of president of the United States, ROMNEY will accept direction to fulfill the promises written about in the above quoted sections. Believing he is doing it for God, He will not hesitate to use his power as commander in chief of the armed forces of the United States and its military-industrial complex to turn the United States into a dictatorship crossing the abyss [Rubicon] feared by Senator Church thus permanently injuring the plaintiffs and their posterity.

31. Plaintiff asserts that the court should issue a Temporary Restraining Order to ROMNEY suspending his campaign for the U.S. Presidency and ordering him to show cause why he should not be permanently enjoined from becoming a candidate again until such time as he removes his membership from the LDS Church and condemns its quest for empire.

31. Plaintiff alleges that in the past he has been in the cross hairs of the sinister side of the LDS "Church". Since the allegations made herein are volatile to the assuaged character and damming to the agenda of the church, the court should order him a

protection plan by the U.S. Marshalls Service pending outcome of these proceedings.

COUNT ONE

32. Plaintiff restates and incorporates all of the above allegations as though fully set forth herein. Defendant Holder has failed and refused to investigate the allegations which have been made concerning the present and imminent dangers concerning threats to the Constitution and the Republic by the construction of the UTAH DATA CENTER. The court should issue a writ of Mandamus to defendant HOLDER mandating that he do due diligence in investigating the allegations of seditious activity which would bar the eligibility of defendant ROMNEY as President.

COUNT TWO

33. Plaintiff restates and incorporates all of the above allegations as though fully set forth herein. The court should issue a writ of mandamus to defendant HALBROOKS requiring her to suspend construction of the UTAH DATA CENTER and investigate the dangers posed by its continued construction as per the allegations of this complaint.

COUNT THREE

34. Plaintiff restates and incorporates all of the above allegations as though fully set forth herein The court should issue a temporary restraining order against defendant ROMNEY temporarily restraining him from further campaigning for the office of President and an order to show cause why he should not be permanently enjoined from seeking that office.

COUNT FOUR

35. Plaintiff restates and incorporates all of the above allegations as though fully set forth herein The injury to the plaintiff and his

class, indeed to the experiment of the Republic of the United States is imminently present should Defendant ROMNEY be allowed to proceed to be elected President of the United States without addressing the alleged issues. How one measures that injury at this point is impossible. The court should preemptively protect against that injury. For if the injury occurs, it will be impossible to salvage the republic because of the technology of the NSA facility then under the control of a theocratic dictatorship in Utah. The Republic would be unable to organize and re-establish itself as per the dire warning of Senator Frank Church.

36. Wherefore Plaintiff asks the court for the following relief:

1. Issue a temporary restraining order against defendant ROMNEY to discontinue his candidacy for president with an order to show cause why he should not be permanently barred from seeking that office.

2. Issue a writ of Mandamus to defendant HOLDER to investigate the allegations of seditious activity of the LDS Church and to do due diligence as to the propriety of the continued construction of the NSA UTAH DATA CENTER under the purview of the historical empire quest of the LDS Church.

3. Issue a writ of mandamus to defendant HALLBROOKS to immediately suspend all construction of the Utah Data Center pending outcome of these proceedings and to investigate the allegations of danger to the government of the United State and its people posed by having the facility available to the seditious organization known as the Mormon Church.

4. Order the US Marshal's Service to provide a protection plan for plaintiff's safety against reprisal for his exposing this corrupt sedition pending outcome of this action.

5. For further or additional relief the court deems appropriate. Plaintiff reserves the right to amend this complaint at any time without motion to the court.

Respectfully submitted this 28 day of March, 2012.

__/S/_____
Douglas A. Wallace. Plaintiff in pro per
Plaintiff affirms he has read this complaint and that it is true and accurate based upon personal knowledge and belief.
DAW
Plaintiff

UPDATE! September 11, 2012

Plaintiff has received notice from the court that the lawsuit will be dismissed without prejudice on or after September 25, 2012 for want of prosecution unless plaintiff can show just cause for the delay. While I can show just cause, I may dismiss against Romney due to the shortness of time to general elections. Political exposure of the Mormon quest will be attempted to deter Americans voting for Romney in swing states.

In any event, if Romney is defeated there will still be a need to pursue the litigation as to the NSA Data Center In Utah and to deter Romney or another Melchizedek Priesthood holder from seeking election in 2016.

Most recent editing November 28, 2012

www.ingramcontent.com/pod-product-compliance
Lightning Source LLC
Chambersburg PA
CBHW071711170526
45165CB00005B/1971